"*Adrian Despres is a real man. It is not his intimidating size as a former football player, but his bold testimony as a follower of Jesus Christ that is impressive. In Christian Man Laws, Adrian challenges men to go to a new dimension beyond athleticism and a macho lifestyle to live with conviction. Filled with humor and practical advice, this book will inspire and guide men to step up to their potential as a husband, a father, a Christian witness and true disciple of Jesus Christ.*"

Jerry Rankin, President Emeritus
International Mission Board, SBC

"*I have known Adrian Despres, our Team Chaplain, for over six years now since I became the football coach at The University of South Carolina. I believe Adrian to be the most sincere, passionate, and persistent preacher that I know. His beliefs, that being a Christian and being a strong, tough, and righteous man, are a blessing to me and our entire football team.*"

Steve Spurrier
Head Football Coach
University of South Carolina

CHRISTIAN MAN LAWS

TIME TO MAN UP

ADRIAN DESPRES

Christian Man Laws
Adrian Despres

Published by Forge, 14485 East Evans Avenue, Denver, Colorado 80014

ISBN 979-8-9854126-3-5 (paperback)
ISBN 979-8-9854126-4-2 (e-book)

Written by Adrian Despres
First printed, 2011

Cover design by Chris Turner

Visit us online at www.forgeforward.org
For more information about Adrian Despres, visit www.adriandespres.com

CONTENTS

INTRODUCTION

MAN UP!

JEROME BETTIS, BURT REYNOLDS, AND SEVEN OTHER MEN ARE seated around a large square table. The younger men obviously fail to command the same presence as their counterparts.

"Men of the square table, is it cool for men to put a lime wedge in their beer?" one of the younger men drawls as he holds up a lime. His other younger friends nod in approval.

"Who knows what they'll put in our beer next?" another man asks. "Banana slices? Kumquats? Where does it end?"

"I'll tell you where it ends. Right here!" a professional wrestler shouts as he pounds the table. "No fruit in beer."

"Don't fruit the beer," an elderly man articulates as he inscribes his words into an oversized, dusty old book.

"Man law?" the wrestler asks.

"Man law!" the rest of the group responds in agreement.

I hate it that beer commercials are so good.

Christian Man Laws

Then it hit me! Christian men need a book of man laws to live by. Laws tailored specifically for men.

I'm sick and tired of men who are sissies for Christ. Men, society has feminized us. We have allowed our masculinity to be taken from us, and we have no one to blame but ourselves. We're not tough enough.

Walking every day with Jesus is HARD. No question about it. It's so much more than doing the typical Sunday morning thing and then you're done. So much more.

Instead of focusing on the negative, let's look at it from a positive perspective. Let's turn the tables and *be* men. Tough. Let's actually risk—R-I-S-K—our lives for Christ.

As men, the key to growing intimate with the Lord is to take risks that require us to "MAN UP" for the cause of Christ. And once we step out, we'll discover that God gives us the power to live for Him.

What do I mean by risk? Risking your reputation, your pride. Sharing your faith. Obeying God's Word. Laying down your life. The risk may not be as great as sharing your faith in the Middle East, but it's still a sacrifice.

Jesus promised that his followers would be persecuted (John 15:20). Second Timothy 3:12 tells us, "Everyone who wants to live a godly life in Christ Jesus will be persecuted." Now that's a man's man. So if we're not being persecuted, we're probably not living manly lives.

Men, it's time to man up.

Women have become the leaders in the church. I'm not saying this is wrong, but I think they're crying out for us to be leaders as well.

God has created and called us to be men. We need to be men for Him.

It's Time to Stand Up!

The purpose of this book is to spur men toward love and good deeds (Hebrews 10:24). To call men who will stand up and be counted.

We have given those in the media the wrong picture of what a Christian man looks like, and they in turn have taken it to its logical extreme.

In the movie *Major League*, the owner of the Cleveland Indians pieces together a team of losers and misfits in hopes they will come in last so she can move the team to Miami. In one scene, the "Christian man" asks to say a prayer before the team takes the field. As the team waits in annoyed silence, he pauses for a moment and then in a wimpy little voice asks God to help them on the field. During his prayer, the pagan baseball player—who worships a god named Jobu—blows up something in his locker, triggering the overhead sprinklers. The movie portrays the Christian as an idiot and the pagan as a hero. But saddest of all, the scene subtly implies that prayer is a waste of time.

This is just one of many similar movie scenes. The media mocks Christians, so men are responding by not taking a stand for Jesus.

But this isn't the true picture of the godly man. The manly Christian man loves his wife, respects others, works hard, shares his faith, and understands who he is in Christ. And this is just the beginning. We need to understand ourselves and follow God's design for our lives as men. We are God's call. God's men. And God wants to use us.

In the same way that you can't drive anywhere in a parked car, God doesn't use men who aren't willing to go where He wants to take them. He probably can if He wants to, but He doesn't.

Paul expresses it this way in Romans 10:14: "How can they believe in the one of whom they have not heard? And how can they hear without someone preaching to them?"

This is the call God has given every one of us.

You have been called, by God, to take His message of love and forgiveness to the world. He's called women, too, but this book is about you, and God spurring you on toward love and good works.

I write this book because men aren't standing up and being the men God has called them to be. At the end of every chapter, I include a section called the "Toolbox." Its purpose is to give you some practical tools to apply the principles in the chapter.

Please understand, I realize that I fall short every day. I'm still a knucklehead. But I'm trying to grow as a man, and this book reflects what God has shown me about what it means to be a man and love God.

You may be hurting. I rarely meet men who don't struggle with low self-esteem or other serious issues. Sin may have entangled your thoughts and life. Don't let these things send you—and keep you—on the sidelines. That's what this book is about.

We need to get back in the game. Too many of us are watching this game called Christianity from the sidelines. Too many of us are sitting at home, on the couch, with a big bag of chips on our bellies and the remote in our hands.

Let's get in the game, guys. Let's learn what it means man up and to be a Christian man.

Let's study the Christian man laws!

CHRISTIAN MAN LAW #1

CHRISTIAN MEN ARE TOUGH

"I'M NOT AFRAID TO KILL YOU! I AIN'T AFRAID TO GO BACK TO prison!" the gang leader shouted as he and his homeys circled around me like sharks sizing up their prey. "You think I'm afraid to stab you? I ain't afraid of nothin'!"

While I was sharing the gospel with some teenagers in a parking lot, a van full of inner city gang members had pulled up and tried to start a fight with some of the guys. I didn't appreciate them getting in the way of sharing the love of Jesus!

"Get out of here," I told them. "Can't you see I'm talking to these guys about Jesus?"

On the other side of the lot my fears were realized when the gang members got out of their van and faced off with the guys who were there. I knew what was going on because I used to fight before I became a Christian. I ran across the parking lot and jumped in the middle of the potential rumble.

"Hey!" I yelled. "Before you fight, let's pray!" Then I closed my eyes. "Dear God, please bless these guys in this fight and don't let them die. But if they *do* die, please don't let them go to hell. Save them right now!"

That's when the gang members began circling me. The gang leader was pretty imposing—about six foot three, thick, and tattooed from head to toe.

I have the gift of discernment, and I discerned that he had just gotten out of prison and that he wasn't afraid of cutting me. He confirmed all of that when he told me he had just been released. Then he double confirmed it when he pulled a knife out of his back pocket and held it against my gut.

What do you say to a guy who was just released from prison and isn't afraid to kill you? If he takes me out, he solidifies his position as the leader of the gang. I was six foot six and a defensive lineman at Furman University at the time. Do the math.

"Go ahead and stab me," I replied, trying to remain calm. "Go ahead. Jesus died for me. Why can't I die for you?"

"Your only chance of knowing what Jesus thinks about you is by stabbing me," I said, as the intensity of my voice began to rise. "Why can't I bleed for you? Jesus bled for me!!!"

Then I screamed, "Cut me!"

"Man, you're weird!" the young man said as he stuck his knife in his back pocket.

"Don't you want to give me a hug?" I asked.

I'm not sure where that came from. But the guy reached up, hugged me, and whispered in my ear, "No one's ever hugged me before."

That night four of those gang members—including that leader —gave their lives to Christ.

We Need Tough Men Who Are Willing to Lay Down Their Lives

Jesus was a man's man, not because He was big but because He was unafraid to lay down His life for others. That's what I call tough!

Jesus said, "Greater love has no one than this, that he lay down his life for his friends" (John 15:13). These weren't empty words. Jesus laid down His life for you and me by dying on a cross.

Jesus also invited His followers to be like Him. He told them (and us), "If anyone would come after me, he must deny himself and take up his cross daily and follow me" (Luke 9:23).

After Jesus ascended to heaven and gave the Holy Spirit to the church, His followers acted the same way. In Acts 5, the religious authorities couldn't get the apostles to be quiet about Jesus. They even threw them in jail, hoping to get them to quit telling people about Jesus. But in the middle of the night an angel unlocked the doors and set them free.

But get this: the angel told them to go preach in the temple courts, just across the street from where they were scheduled to stand trial (Acts 5:20).

That's what I call tough!

So the authorities brought them before the religious court (called the Sanhedrin) and ordered the men to be flogged, which means they were whipped on their backs thirty-nine times. Then they were ordered not to preach anymore about Jesus.

After the pain and hassle of sharing their faith about Jesus, you'd think they'd be a little more careful. Not on your life!

The apostles left the Sanhedrin, rejoicing because they had been counted worthy of suffering disgrace for the Name. Day after day, in the temple courts and from house to house, they never stopped teaching and proclaiming the good news that Jesus is the Christ. Acts 5:41–42

The apostles rejoiced because they had been beaten for Jesus' sake!!!!

The apostle Paul was no different. He wrote to the church in Philippi, "It has been *granted* to you on behalf of Christ not only to believe on him, but also to suffer for him" (Philippians 1:29, italics added).

The Greek word translated as "granted" here can also be translated "given generously." Suffering is a gift from God, just like salvation!

Paul understood suffering. In 2 Corinthians he wrote, "Five times I received from the Jews the forty lashes minus one" (2 Corinthians 11:24). That's misleading, though. He didn't receive just thirty-nine lashes. The strap the Jews used to whip Jesus had three more straps at the end. If you multiply 3 leather straps times 39 strikes, you get 117 lashes for every beating. Remember, Paul said he was beaten 5 times, so that makes 585 lashes.

We also know that Paul was flogged at least once with a cat-of-nine-tails by the Romans (Acts 16:22-23). This especially cruel whip was split into nine leather straps. According to archaeological findings, each leather strap was baked in clay with pieces of sharp metal or sharpened bones fastened every four inches. In addition, rocks or other ball-like objects were attached between the metal or bones. So the rocks bruised the muscles while the sharp metal tore the skin. Not only that, but the lash hit the back and then whipped around to the other side, tearing open both the front and back of the victim. The person was mercilessly beaten from the bottom of the neck to the top of the knee.

But that doesn't come close to the many sufferings Paul experienced. If you want to read more, just turn to 2 Corinthians 11:23-33.

Shortly after this description of his sufferings in chapter 11, Paul remarks, "That is why, for Christ's sake, I delight in weaknesses, in insults, in hardships, in persecutions, in difficulties. For when I am weak, then I am strong" (2 Corinthians 12:10).

That's tough, guys. And God called Christian men to be tough. It's a Man Law.

Passion Is the Key to Toughness

Why are so few men willing to risk their lives for the cause of Christ? Because they lack passion.

My wife, Lisa, provides a great example of passion. She loves to shop. For me, ten minutes in a mall and my right leg starts to go numb. My eyes lose focus and the world becomes hazy. I seriously can't take it. It borders on torture.

Contrast that with the fact that Lisa and her girlfriends go on a spiritual retreat every year at a mall outside of Charlotte, North Carolina. They spend two days shopping and talking about Jesus in the food court. I don't get it, but Lisa comes home energized and revived. If she dragged me with her I think I would die of SSE—shopping stroke exhaustion.

My wife is passionate about shopping. I call it suffering. That is what passion does; it makes suffering look like entertainment. Let me explain.

What are men passionate about? Sports. Cars. Hunting. Fishing. Tons of stuff.

Take bow hunting, for example. Men will wake up in the middle of the night and sit for hours in a tree stand they can barely squeeze into, waiting for a deer. And they'll refuse to move—even if a mosquito gets under their net and sucks them dry. They don't want to scare away the deer. If you've ever gone deer hunting, you know exactly what I mean.

Other men will show up at church on Sunday morning with a face redder than a fire engine because they spent Saturday afternoon at State U's football game. Suffering means little when it involves your passions. In fact, it makes suffering look like entertainment.

My friend Carl is a national strongman champion. He weighs 200 pounds in order to stay in his weight class, but the guy's a monster. He can't hold his arms down at his side because they're so big. Carl can squat 4 sets of 12 repetitions at 405 pounds!

So one morning he comes up to me after a workout, veins popping out everywhere, and says, "Adrian, now THAT'S a good burn."

I started laughing. A "good burn"? What in the world is a good burn? Only people who want to get stronger say that. You've heard the phrase "No pain, no gain." That's exactly what a good burn is all about.

You can tell what you love by the pain you're willing to experience in order to enjoy it. You may even consider it entertainment. You love the pain! You want the pain! Because you know what it's leading toward.

The word *passion* comes from the Latin word *pati*, which literally means "to suffer." Passion and suffering go together. That's why we call the sacrifice Jesus made for us on the cross the "passion" of Jesus. It's His suffering. Hebrews 12:2 tells us that Jesus "for the joy set before him endured the cross."

Why are there so few people today willing to suffer for Jesus? Because they lack passion for *Him*.

And where can we get a passion for Jesus? The passage we just read from Hebrews gives us a clue. Here is Hebrews 12:2 in its entirety:

Let us fix our eyes on Jesus, the author and perfecter of our faith, who for the joy set before him endured the cross, scorning its shame, and sat down at the right hand of the throne of God.

When these word were written, the church was beginning to suffer persecution. Slowly losing strength, the believers needed an injection of passion to keep them going. So the author told them fix their eyes on Jesus.

The Greek word for *fix* means to immerse yourself in something. So to fix your thoughts on Jesus means to immerse yourself in Him: How did Jesus suffer? How have *you* inflicted the same kind of suffering on Him? How does Jesus respond to suffering? Imagine Jesus joyfully dying on the cross for *your* sins.

You see, suffering becomes a joy when it involves what—or who—we love. When we understand the depths of God's love for us, we willingly and joyfully lay down our lives for Him.

Our passions are also a product of our will. Love is a choice; so when we choose to love God, our passions follow like the caboose on a train. And when we love Him, we're willing to suffer joyfully for Him too. This comes through in Paul's letter to the Romans:

 We rejoice in the hope of the glory of God. Not only so, but we also rejoice in our sufferings, because we know that suffering produces perseverance; perseverance, character; and character, hope. And hope does not disappoint us, because God has poured out his love into our hearts by the Holy Spirit, whom he has given us.

ROMANS 5:2-5

Believe It or Not, Passion, Joy, and Suffering Go Together

A friend of mine tried to share the gospel with a bunch of teenagers who were throwing beer bottles on the ground in a parking lot. While talking to one of them, another kid snuck behind him and tried to take his wallet. Then another one slammed his jaw with a bottle. Falling backward into the bushes, he saw stars (not those little birdies you see in cartoons —they lied to us!), many stars.

As the guys ran to their car to grab some clubs so they could beat him, my friend jumped to his feet to protect himself. When they ran back, the guy who had just pummeled him asked, "Why are you here?"

"I came here to tell you guys about Jesus!" my friend replied.

Immediately the young man dropped his beer bottle on the ground, walked behind his car, and laid his head on the trunk. The rest of the guys put their clubs away and excitedly ran up to my friend.

"We all ran away from home tonight," one of the boys explained. "But while you were talking, all of us heard something inside tell us that we should go home. Do you think God spoke to us? Is that possible?"

That night my friend prayed with those teens to give their lives to Christ—and they all went home.

When you're passionate for Jesus, you'll gladly suffer for him. That's what I call tough!

 TOOL BOX

So how do you get tough?

1. Fix your eyes on Jesus.

- Spend time studying how Jesus suffered for you. Matthew 26:36–27:61; Mark 14:32–15:47; Luke 22:39–23:56; John 18:1–19:42. Then ask yourself: How did Jesus suffer? How have *I* inflicted the same kind of suffering on Him? How did Jesus respond to suffering? Imagine Jesus joyfully dying on the cross for *your* sins.
- Watch the movie *The Passion of the Christ*.
- List as many of your sins as you can on a sheet of paper. Then, in red ink, write over your list, "Jesus died for my sins. I'll live for Him."

2. Live tough. The only way you can be tough is by making toughness an active part of your life. Make a list of things you can do to obey God radically. Here are some examples:

- Cut your neighbor's grass.

- Compliment your wife on how she looks.
- Ask your boss or employees how you can serve them.
- Share your faith.

3. Remember that all struggles are training. When you fall, get back up—but remember why you fell so it won't happen again. God is preparing your heart for something bigger with every trial. You don't need to suffer in vain.

4. Meditate on the following passages about persecution and suffering:

> James 1:2-4: "Consider it pure joy, my brothers, whenever you face trials of many kinds, because you know that the testing of your faith develops perseverance. Perseverance must finish its work so that you may be mature and complete, not lacking anything."

> Romans 5:3-5: "We also rejoice in our sufferings, because we know that suffering produces perseverance; perseverance, character; and character, hope. And hope does not disappoint us, because God has poured out his love into our hearts by the Holy Spirit, whom he has given us."

> Matthew 5:11-12: "Blessed are you when people insult you, persecute you and falsely say all kinds of evil against you because of me. Rejoice and be glad, because great is your reward in heaven, for in the same way they persecuted the prophets who were before you."

When you encounter persecution, you stand alongside men like Jeremiah, Isaiah, and Moses. These words of Jesus from

Matthew 5:11-12 completely changed my mind about my circumstances one night after some female peers made fun of me for following Him. I call this a "gut shot." These verses came to mind in my apartment later that night, and I started to dance and then pray for those ladies. When they needed a ride the next day, I was glad to give them one. I got the last laugh, however, because they gave their hearts to Christ!

———

Let me leave you with these words: If you decide to follow Jesus with all your heart, it is going to cost you everything. If you decide not to follow Him with all your heart, it is still going to cost you everything. The only difference is who gets your everything: Satan, who hates your guts and wants you ruined, miserable, and dead—or Jesus, who loves you and wants you joyful, successful, and thriving. The choice is yours.

CHRISTIAN MAN LAW #2

CHRISTIAN MEN KNOW WHO THEY ARE

A COUPLE OF YEARS AGO I OFFICIATED AT A WEDDING FOR SOME friends. During the ceremony I asked the couple, "Did you know that God is especially fond of you?" Then I quoted David's words in Psalm 139:17-18: "How precious to me are your thoughts, O God! How vast is the sum of them! Were I to count them, they would outnumber the grains of sand."

I went on to mention that a scientist once counted the number of grains in a cubic foot of sand and then estimated how many cubic feet of sand was on the earth. His estimate included the ocean shore lines, the ocean floors, and inland sand. He concluded that the number of grains of sand on the earth was 1×10^{27}. For the mathematically challenged, that's 1 with 27 zeroes after it.

"That's the number of precious thoughts God has about you," I told the couple.

Afterward, a national champion football coach who attended the ceremony shook my hand and said, "Adrian, your comments about God being fond of the couple really spoke to me." For the next few moments I shared more with the coach about God's love for him.

I often use the word *fond*, because the word *love* has worn thin over the years. Even the phrase "Jesus loves you" has lost its impact. So, by replacing *love* with *fond*, the message has regained its power.

Think about it for a moment: God is especially fond of you. That means not only that He loves you, but that His heart is warmed when He thinks of you.

Why Are Men Insecure?

Most men I know are insecure. They may come across as funny, self-confident, or cocky, but inside they're afraid, ashamed, and suffer from low self-esteem. And they struggle to believe that God is fond of them.

Low self-esteem has harassed me all my life. In order to convince people to like me, I excelled in sports. The harder I worked, the more people seemed to like me—which made me work even harder.

That mindset dominated my life; but eventually, trying to get people to like me burned me out. No one can do that forever, because 1) it requires a great deal of energy, and 2) getting everyone to like you is virtually impossible. Plus, wanting people to like you is rooted in pride.

But a Christian man who knows who he is in Christ doesn't need to be funny all the time or act self-confident or cocky. He can be the man God has created him to be.

That's why Christian Man Law #2 is "Christian men know who they are." They know who they are in Christ because they know Christ is in them. Let me explain ...

The Power of Knowing That Christ Lives in You

Years ago while sitting in a seminary class, my professor, Dr. Brad Mullen, showed us a series of slides that shook me in my inner man and forever changed me. His presentation impacted me so deeply that I sobbed for a half-hour. I couldn't believe that what I saw was true.

This is what he shared.

ADAM BEFORE THE FALL

This is Adam before he sinned. He and Ever were the most perfect people ever to live, other than Jesus. Because neither of them had sinned, they enjoyed an intimate relationship with God. Apparently they walked with God in the garden, because after they sinned they recognized the sound of God walking in the garden (Genesis 3:8).

ADAM AFTER THE FALL

The next illustration represents Adam and Eve after they sinned. Notice that the circle is empty because God has separated Himself from the couple. He no longer lives in them. Sin has completely marred them—and the squiggly line is a vine that represents sin. The arrows point up, which means that sin has dominion over their lives. In theological terms, we would say that they are "depraved." Their natural inclination to sin is called the "sin nature."

NORMAL CHRISTIAN

This is the normal Christian. Society might consider this person "radical" or "on fire," but the Bible considers someone like this normal. Notice that sin still persists, but not in a dominant fashion. The vines of sin exist, but now the arrows point down, because sin no longer has dominion. The normal Christian is capable of sinning, but it's not natural.

Now let's examine what is inside the circle . . .

As Dr. Mullen began explaining what was inside the circle, I started sobbing. I had trouble believing that he could be showing me who I am.

What's inside the circle? You may not be ready yet for this truth, so let's set it up!!

The Extreme Measure of God

Inside the circle represents the fact that God goes to extreme measures to bring the lost to Himself. Did you catch that?

God goes to extreme measures to bring the lost to Himself.

In 1 Kings 18, Elijah challenged the prophets of Baal and Asherah to a competition to prove who was the true God. It was Elijah versus 850 false prophets. Because I like college football, I picture this happening on a Saturday afternoon—with Elijah playing the wide receiver.

Elijah instructed the prophets and onlookers—people from all over Israel—that fire from heaven would light the sacrifice of the true God. Then he gave them permission to go first. He knew nothing would happen because their gods had no power.

All morning long the 850 prophets danced around their altar, but nothing happened. Then at noon Elijah stepped forward and taunted them. "Shout louder!" he said. "Surely he is a god! Perhaps he is deep in thought, or busy, or traveling. Maybe he is sleeping and must be awakened" (verse 27).

This is hilarious, because the Hebrew word for *busy* means using the bathroom!

Unable to convince their gods to cooperate, the prophets got frantic and started cutting themselves. They shouted louder, hoping to bring the wrath of their gods on Elijah. I like what the Bible says next: "But there was no response, no one answered, no one paid attention" (verse 29).

Smart aleck Elijah allowed this to continue another six hours, for a total of around ten hours. Can you see the prophets lying on the ground, completely worn out?!

Then Elijah repaired the altar of God, laid a slaughtered bull on it, and doused it with water three times. Remember the deal between Elijah and the false prophets: the true God would prove His existence by burning up the sacrifice. So why was Elijah making it hard on God? He wasn't! He was making it apparent that only God could light the fire—not some stray match stick.

Then Elijah prayed, "Answer me, O Lord, answer me, so [these people] will know that you, O Lord, are God, and that *you are turning their hearts back again*" (verse 37, italics added).

Immediately, fire from heaven fell and consumed all the meat, the stones, the wood, the water, even the dirt. Then all the people turned back to God, saying "The Lord—he is God! The Lord—he is God!" (verse 39).

God goes to extreme measures to bring the lost to Himself!

Take the cross, for example. In college, I wrote my senior thesis about the physical suffering Jesus experienced on the cross. The doctors I studied said that crucifixion is one of the most painful forms of torture known to humankind!

God goes to extreme measures to bring the lost to Himself.

I call it the Extreme Measure of God.

You **Are the Extreme Measure of God!**

Now let's look at what's inside of the circle in the illustration.

NORMAL CHRISTIAN

Colossians 1:26-27 says,

> [This is] the mystery that has been kept hidden for ages and generations, but is now disclosed to the saints. To them God has chosen to make known among the Gentiles the glorious riches of this mystery, which is *Christ in you, the hope of glory* (italics added).

Christ lives in you!!! The infinite God has chosen to take up residence within you!!

You are more powerful than you could ever imagine. You are the Extreme Measure of God to bring the lost to Himself.

Even if your self-esteem is the size of a toothpick—you're a toothpick duct-taped to a lead pipe!!! Christ lives in you!

You are the Extreme Measure of God!

NORMAL CHRISTIAN

In Ephesians 1:13-14, Paul writes,

> You also were included in Christ when you heard the word of truth, the gospel of your salvation. Having believed, you were marked in him with a seal, the promised Holy Spirit, who is a deposit guaranteeing our inheritance until the redemption of those who are God's possession.

Not only does Christ live in you, the Holy Spirit lives in you as well.

But that's not all—there's more!

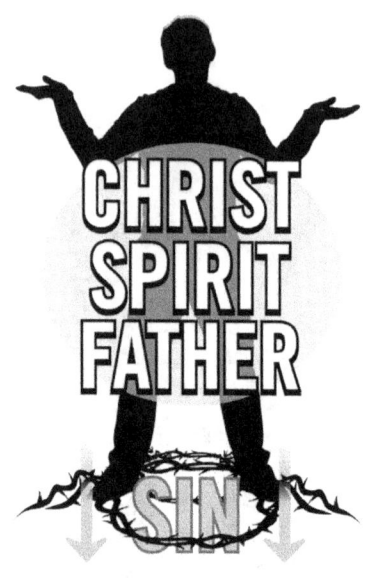

NORMAL CHRISTIAN

Jesus said,

> If anyone loves me, he will obey my teaching. My Father will love him, and we will come to him and make our home with him."
>
> JOHN 14:23

That means God the Father has taken up residence in you, too.

If you have given your heart to Jesus, then every member of the Trinity lives in you! You are amazing!!

Now compare the first illustration with the last one . . .

ADAM BEFORE THE FALL   NORMAL CHRISTIAN

Something has been restored. God now dwells in us just like he did in Adam and Eve before they sinned.

You're more powerful than you think. When we say something about God to someone, all of the authority of heaven stands behind us.

This Is Who You Are!

Let's look at a few more biblical truths concerning who we are in Christ.

How great is the love the Father has lavished on us, that we should be called children of God! And that is what we are! 1 John 3:1

I love the word *lavish*. Here's what I see when I read that word.

I love to eat. I think food is a blessing from God. A big stack of pancakes? Gift from God.

What does it mean to lavish?

Imagine a big stack of steaming pancakes. Butter slowly melting on top. Then you begin pouring syrup over the pancakes. All that syrupy goodness engulfs the butter and begins running down the sides. But you keep pouring. The syrup fills up the edge of your plate and flows onto the table. Soon the entire surface is covered, so that nectar from heaven slowly surges onto the floor, forming a pool around your feet. Suddenly you're knee-deep in syrup.

That's what I call lavishing your pancakes with syrup.

This is a glimpse of how the Father has lavished us with His love!! God's love never tasted so good!

Not only has God lavished you with His love, but He has chosen you:

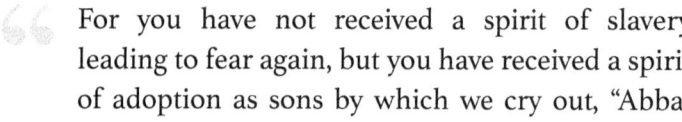

> For you have not received a spirit of slavery leading to fear again, but you have received a spirit of adoption as sons by which we cry out, "Abba! Father!"
>
> ROMANS 8:15 (NASB)

Do you know what it means to be adopted? I was raised by my biological parents, so I don't fully understand it. But adoption means you've been chosen and given the full rights of a biological son or daughter.

> The Spirit Himself testifies with our spirit that we are children of God. And if children, heirs also, heirs of God and fellow heirs with Christ.

> ROMANS 8:16-17 (NASB)

The word *if* can also be translated *since*. In this particular context the word should clearly be translated *since*, because we are identified as children of God in the previous verse.

That word *since* is extremely important. *Since* means "beyond a shadow of a doubt." It's a done deal.

Also notice that verse 17 speaks of "heirs of God and fellow heirs with Christ." The King James Version uses the phrase "joint-heirs with Christ." You are joined to Christ. I don't know if you can get ahold of that in your thinking... you are a joint-heir *with* Christ.

God has adopted you and given you an inheritance—which is what heirs receive. He

didn't adopt you so you could be his lowly servant, like a male version of Cinderella. He gave you the rights and privileges of his one and only son, Jesus Christ!

Here's the last juicy morsel I want to throw your way:

> For in Christ all the fullness of the Deity lives in bodily form, and you have been given fullness in Christ, who is the head over every power and authority.

> COLOSSIANS 2:9-10

The *fullness* of Christ dwells in you. The word *fullness* means "complete." Everything you read about Jesus in the Bible dwells in you. It makes me want to sing that early 90s song, "I've Got the Power"!

Think about the first car you owned. If you're like me, it probably wasn't all that nice. My first car was a Chevy Nova. Know what *Nova* means in Spanish? "No go." What a great description of my first car!

Unfortunately, that's the way most of us view ourselves. We think we're a broken-down piece of machinery. Worn out and beaten down. We look at ourselves as junk, scrap metal—when we're really a Mercedes, Lexus, or Rolls-Royce. That's who you are.

The Father, Son, and Holy Spirit live in you!

 TOOL BOX

1. Spend some time meditating on the following statements and looking up the corresponding verses. I would not study them all in one day but refer back to them over several days. If you have given your life to Jesus, then these are the deepest truths about you:

- You are loved by God (Romans 1:7).

- You are justified (Romans 5:1). In other words, God looks at you as if you've never sinned.

- You have been saved from God's wrath (Romans 5:9).

- You have been reconciled to God (Romans 5:10).

- You have new life (Romans 6:4).

- You have been united with Christ in His resurrection (Romans 6:5).

- You have been freed from sin (Romans 6:6-7).

- You are dead to sin (Romans 6:11).

- You are alive to God (Romans 6:11).

- You are no longer condemned (Romans 8:1).

- You are controlled by the Spirit, not the sinful nature (Romans 8:9).

- You are a child of God (Romans 8:15-16).

- You are a co-heir with Christ (Romans 8:17).

- God is working all things together in your life for your good (Romans 8:28).

- God has freely given you all things (Romans 8:32).

- Nothing can separate you from God's love (Romans 8:39).

- You are sanctified in Christ Jesus (1 Corinthians 1:2). This means you are no longer a sinner saved by grace —you're a saint who occasionally sins.

- You have the mind of Christ (1 Corinthians 2:16).

- You are God's temple (1 Corinthians 6:19).

- You are the aroma of Christ (2 Corinthians 2:15).

- You are a new creation (2 Corinthians 5:17).

- You are Christ's ambassador (2 Corinthians 5:20).

2. Study Ephesians, Philippians, and Colossians and create a list of what they say about you.

CHRISTIAN MAN LAW #3

CHRISTIAN MEN CULTIVATE FERTILE HEARTS

Do you know what an oxymoron is? It's a word or phrase that contradicts itself. They've become so commonplace that we hear and say them without a second thought. But, guys, stop for a second and consider some of these mixed messages:

- Bittersweet
- Upside down
- Pretty ugly (That one made me laugh when I wrote it right then)
- Icy hot

One of my football coaches in college used to say, "Hurry up and take a break."

How about "deafening silence"?
"Friendly fire"?
"Good grief"?
"Jumbo shrimp"?
"Committed Christian"?

Oops, did I just say that? Is calling someone a "committed Christian" an oxymoron?

Do you know how most people define what it means to be a Christian today? By church attendance. If you go to church three Sundays a month, you're clearly committed. Four Sundays a month, and you're committed more than most. One or two Sundays a month is all right. The C & E people? That means they show up on Christmas and Easter. Uh, their walk with Christ isn't all that great, but they're Christians nevertheless.

Even though church attendance is important, it doesn't serve as an accurate indicator of your commitment to Christ. Your walk with Christ is based on what you do *after* church, throughout the week. How you live between the time you leave church until you return the next week—not what you do while you're sitting in a pew—determines your commitment.

The Four Soils

Jesus told a parable in Matthew 13 that describes what I'm talking about. I call it "The Parable of the Four Soils," but it's also known as "The Parable of the Sower."

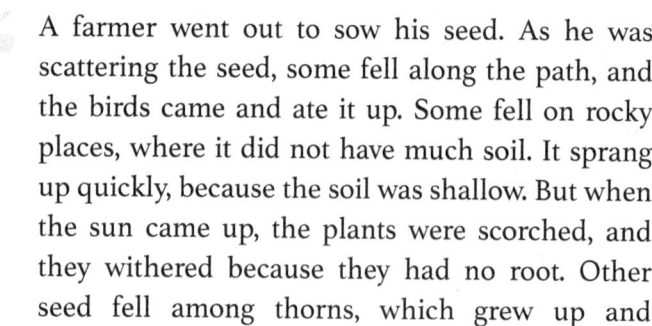

> A farmer went out to sow his seed. As he was scattering the seed, some fell along the path, and the birds came and ate it up. Some fell on rocky places, where it did not have much soil. It sprang up quickly, because the soil was shallow. But when the sun came up, the plants were scorched, and they withered because they had no root. Other seed fell among thorns, which grew up and

choked the plants. Still other seed fell on good soil, where it produced a crop—a hundred, sixty or thirty times what was sown. He who has ears, let him hear.

MATTHEW 13:3-9

One seed, four soils. Obviously, the only variable that produces a harvest—the key element within our control—is the soil.

Soil #1: *Calloused Hearts*

The first soil in Jesus' parable could hardly be described as soil, because people walked on it so often that it became a path. The seed sown on the path never really had a chance to take root since the ground was so hard. You can't expect a harvest from seeds that are scattered on a sidewalk.

After Jesus presented the parable of the four soils to the crowd, He pulled His disciples aside to explain what it meant. This is extremely helpful for us.

> Listen then to what the parable of the sower means: When anyone hears the message about the kingdom and does not understand it, the evil one comes and snatches away what was sown in his heart. This is the seed sown along the path.

MATTHEW 13:18-19

The seed is the message about the kingdom, which includes the gospel or any kernel of truth about the kingdom of God. So when people who resemble the first soil hear the message, they fail to understand it because Satan comes and snatches away the seed.

Jesus described the people in the crowd as always hearing but never understanding, due to the fact that their hearts had become calloused (Matthew 13:14-15). That sounds like the first soil, doesn't it?

That's also a perfect description of modern American culture. Because so many people's hearts have become calloused, very few men today are *biblically* committed to Christ. You can share the gospel with most men all day long, but the seeds never take root.

While talking to a group of Mormon missionaries one time, I explained who Jesus is and showed them—using their own documents—how Joseph Smith was a false prophet. But even after giving them fact after indisputable fact, they still failed to understand. The seed was snatched away.

Of the dozens and dozens of Mormon missionaries with whom I've shared the gospel, not one has given his life to Christ. That breaks my heart. I've led a few Mormons to Christ, but not one Mormon missionary.

This hardheartedness certainly isn't limited to Mormons. You may have family members, friends, or coworkers who have heard the gospel but failed to understand it. Their hearts have become calloused to the conviction of the Holy Spirit. Talking to them about Jesus is like talking to a wall. Or throwing seeds on a sidewalk.

Look closely at how Jesus ends His parable: "He who has ears, let him hear" (Matthew 13:9). He's stepping out of the parable to implore His listeners not to just listen to His words but to open their ears and truly understand those words.

Since you're reading this book, I doubt that you fit into this first group. Your interest demonstrates that, at some level, you care about your relationship with Christ. But you likely know people who need to open their ears and eyes.

Soil #2: The Great Deception

As we'll see in the fourth soil, the amount of fruit produced is the key element of this parable. Because fruit isn't mentioned in conjunction with the second soil, whereas it plays such a big role in relation to the fourth soil, we can assume that no fruit was evident in the second soil—especially since this soil produced few, if any, roots. Some people base their walk with Christ on something they have done in the past without any evidence of long-term change. With the second soil, Jesus is saying that long-term change will always accompany salvation. This is a very dangerous soil for Americans today!!

Jesus described the second soil like this:

 The one who received the seed that fell on rocky places is the man who hears the word and at once receives it with joy. But since he has no root, he lasts only a short time. When trouble or persecution comes because of the word, he quickly falls away.

MATTHEW 13:20-21

When a man's heart resembles the rocky soil, he hears the message and receives it with joy. He grows quickly at first, but that growth lasts only a short time because he isn't *rooted* in the soil.

Many people base their salvation on the occasion of their baptism or confirmation. While these are very positive and important events, they cannot save you apart from a sincere commitment to Christ.

Baptism makes you a Christian about as much as walking into a hamburger joint makes you a hamburger. Seriously, baptism has nothing to do with your salvation. Baptism is the *result* of your salvation, an outward expression of something happening inside you. But the water won't save anyone.

Men whose hearts resemble the rocky places receive the word with joy; but as soon as problems hit, their faith comes crashing down. Perhaps they prayed to receive Christ or joined a church or decided to get baptized because someone else talked them into it. Or maybe they thought it was the thing to do. Or perhaps they hoped it would be good for business.

It is extremely dangerous to make spiritual assumptions. Our country is filled with people who believe they are saved and going to heaven—but they aren't, and they don't even know it!!

Jesus referred to people like this in what I believe is one of the most sobering passages in the Bible:

 Not everyone who says to me, "Lord, Lord," will enter the kingdom of heaven, but only he who does the will of my Father who is in heaven. Many will say to me on that day, "Lord, Lord, did we not prophesy in your name, and in your name drive out demons and perform many miracles?" Then I will tell them plainly, "I never knew you. Away from me, you evildoers!"

MATTHEW 7:21-23

Many men have prayed to receive Jesus but have never truly surrendered themselves to Him. Without surrendering to Jesus, they haven't received the gift of salvation; and as a result, they won't bear any fruit. Salvation must be accompanied by fruit!

And what does this fruit look like? Fruit is your faith in action. The fruit of the Spirit is the actions of the Spirit, which Paul describes as love, joy, peace, patience, kindness, goodness, faithfulness, gentleness, and self-control (Galatians 5:22-23).

James wrote that faith without works is dead (James 2:26). Our works—our fruit—prove that we are saved.

Martin Luther explained it this way: "Faith alone saves you, but faith is never alone."

The rocky soil produces no fruit because persecution and the troubles of life limit its root system.

Do you have any fruit? If not, perhaps your "soil" is rocky and the Holy Spirit needs to plow it up! Ask Him if that's the condition of your heart.

God can change rocky soil!

Soil #3: Inoculated by the Gospel

Jesus then explained people whose hearts resembled the thorny soil:

> The one who received the seed that fell among the thorns is the man who hears the word, but the worries of this life and the deceitfulness of wealth choke it, making it unfruitful.
>
> MATTHEW 13:22

The thorny soil and rocky soil are very similar. The big difference between them boils down to what chokes the seed. Persecution and adversity strangle the seeds planted in the second soil. But with the third type of soil, worries about life and the deceitfulness of wealth choke the seed.

A rich young man once asked Jesus, "What good thing must I do to get eternal life?" (Matthew 19:16).

Jesus answered by pointing out the one obstacle that stood in the way between the man and God: "If you want to be perfect, go, sell your possessions and give to the poor, and you will have treasure in heaven. Then come, follow me"(Matthew 19:21).

Unfortunately, we read that the man walked away very sad, because his wealth was more important to him than eternal life.

As with the second soil, people who resemble the thorny soil often have been talked into their faith without surrendering to Christ. If someone can talk them into it, someone can talk them out of it.

Hanging around Christianity without surrendering to it causes people to be inoculated with gospel. What do I mean by that?

Before traveling to Africa one time, I was required to get a yellow fever shot. Guess what color the liquid inside the needle was.

Yellow! It was yellow!

As the nurse began aiming her needle at my arm, I asked her, "What's that?" I was a little concerned that something was about to go terribly wrong.

"Yellow fever," she answered. "We need to give you enough yellow fever so you build an immunity against it."

When you receive an inoculation, you receive just enough of the disease so your body can build an immunity against it. That's what happens with the third soil. People grow up in church and are exposed to *just* enough Christianity that they build an immunity against it.

When high school kids who grew up in church go to college, as many as 88 percent stop going to church. You may be one of them. Many of these "dropouts" were forced to go to church when they were young. Once they break free from their parents, they break free from the burden of going to church.

Then, when they get married and start having kids, they say to each other, *You know, we should have our kids in church since we were raised in church.* So they come back, usually around age twenty-six. This is especially true in the Bible Belt.

Church, however, is nothing more to them than a country club. They join because society tells them it's the thing to do, that it's important. It's an opportunity to socialize, build their business, or show off their new car or fancy clothes. Like the rich young ruler, wealth has deceived them into believing that this life is more important than eternal life.

Don't get me wrong—going to church isn't wrong. But if you think you're saved by going to church, you're in danger. Big-time danger.

Do you *own* your relationship with Jesus? What I mean is, are you in a relationship with Jesus by your own choice or for some other reason?

I dare you to own your walk with Christ. I dare you to surpass your parents!! Don't let the deceit and worries of this world choke your seed and choke the message of the kingdom. Don't have a thorny heart.

Soil #4: Fruitfulness

Ah, now let's get to the good part. Let's talk about the fourth soil, the good soil, and what that means.

> But the one who received the seed that fell on good soil is the man who hears the word and understands it. He produces a crop, yielding a hundred, sixty or thirty times what was sown.
>
> MATTHEW 13:23

When a man's heart resembles the good soil, he hears the Word of God and understands it. He lets it sink in. This is why it's imperative that we *understand* the Word of God.

Jesus said, "You will know the truth, and the truth will set you free" (John 8:32). The truth doesn't set us free; it's *knowing* the truth that sets us free. What good is the truth if we don't know it and understand it? Too many people misinterpret this verse.

Now look at the last part of Matthew 13:23. Jesus said that seeds planted in the good soil produce a crop thirty, sixty, even a hundred times what was sown. Although I'm fighting everything inside to say it, I'll settle for the thirty times. I'd prefer a hundredfold return, but I'll settle for thirty.

Certain kinds of Babylonian seed produce a crop two hundred times what was sown. Maybe some of you can do that. Jesus wasn't exaggerating when He said this. We need to influence other people directly. The point of this book isn't so much that you can be changed; the point is that you can impact others.

Fruitfulness is the point here—the actions, or fruit, of the Holy Spirit, like I mentioned earlier, and also making an impact on people's lives for the kingdom of God. We don't go to church to get blessed. We go to church so we can be trained and spurred on and encouraged to make disciples of the world. To love God and to love people! To be the Christian men God is calling us to be!! More important than what we do at church is what we do between the time we walk out the door and when we walk back in.

We've missed this point for entirely too long. It's time to man up, understand the soil types, and reach souls for Christ.

My friend Brian attends a weekly Bible study that I lead. He's an impressive man. Not only is he physically strong, but he's also a very successful businessman. (And he is good-looking too, dang it!)

One week I asked Brian, when he gave his life to Christ. "I grew up in church," he replied, "so I've always had a relationship with Jesus."

"Now understand," I explained, "you don't need to know the exact date; but you should have a pretty good idea about when you meet someone very important, like the president of the United States."

I didn't know it at the time, but Brian got really mad. In fact, he didn't return to Bible study for three weeks. When he finally came back, I pulled him aside and asked him again about when he got saved. Right there, with about forty men watching, he said he wasn't sure when it happened and wasn't sure that it had ever happened. So I asked him if he wanted to get saved right then and there.

The room became dead quiet as this tough man's man bowed his head and started to tremble. He prayed right there to give everything to Jesus.

Well, that happened several years ago, and Brian is still an amazing lover of Jesus. Since then he has led many people to Christ—and he's nothing like the loud, obnoxious evangelist writing this book! Brian doesn't have the gift of evangelism; he is simply an ordinary man who loves Jesus.

And he is producing fruit—hundredfold fruit!!

Countless men in the United States and around the world love their wives, tithe, and give generously beyond their tithe for the cause of Christ. They seek God in order to discover what He wants them to do—and then they do it. They have fertile hearts!

How is your heart?

 **TOOL BOX**

How do we cultivate a fertile heart? As men, we need to do two things:

> **Trust**—because we can only walk with God if He helps us. And He loves to help us! He loves it so much that He gave us His Son!!

> **Obey**—because He is worth obeying. This is risky business for us, men. But this is truly the key to the Christian life.

Men, let's get after it!!

CHRISTIAN MAN LAW #4

CHRISTIAN MEN ARE TOUGH ON SIN

ONE NIGHT YEARS AGO, BACK IN MY DAYS AS A SEMINARY STUDENT, my heart started beating in my tooth. Ever felt that? We were too poor to pay attention, so I didn't go to a dentist; and as a result I developed a hole in my tooth that you could shove three toothpicks through. I enjoyed that, because food would get caught in there and I could pick it out later and enjoy it some more.

But it also hurt. Really bad. Especially at night. So I drove to the store and bought some Anbesol (that gel stuff you use for a toothache).

When my toothache woke me up that night, I reached for my pain killer and gave it a shot; but the Anbesol didn't even touch it.

Then I remembered how every athlete treats an injury—so I walked to the refrigerator and pulled out an ice-cube tray. I rubbed one cube on my jaw, and it worked! I went back to sleep until my tooth thawed out five minutes later. That night I went through two ice-cube trays. When I woke up in my prayer chair the next morning, my pajamas were soaked, the chair was soaked, and the carpet was soaked!

The pain in my tooth was off the charts. Then my wife reminded me that a dentist friend had offered to give me free dental work while I was in seminary. Although his office was an hour and a half away, the pain was so bad I was willing to go just about anywhere.

Like most seminary students, we didn't have any money and our car was in bad shape. The power windows in our car were broken, the air conditioner didn't work, and the heater never shut off. To make matters worse, we were suffering through the middle of the hottest summer ever in the Southeast. The day I drove to the dentist, the temperature was around 105 degrees with 98 percent humidity.

When I opened the car door, a hot wind rushed out at me like I was checking out a cherry pie baking in an oven. But it didn't smell near as good. Actually, when I opened the door it smelled like somebody had died.

So I drove down the highway with the door partly open and my head sticking out so I could breathe. Then I'd nod off (because I hadn't slept the night before) in between heart beats, before being rudely awakened by the pain in my tooth.

The dentist x-rayed my tooth and told me it had abscessed. Can I get a witness? The pain felt like giving birth—but I better leave that one alone (in case any women are reading this!). He said he needed to give me a root canal.

"No way," I told him as stood up from my chair. "I'm allergic to pain."

He told me to sit down, then he stuck me eight times to deaden the area!

He drilled three holes in my tooth and then slammed these needles called "reamers" into the holes. I thought he was trying to start a fire in there. It smelled awful, like my car. By the time he started on the third hole, he said he needed to work from a different angle, which led him to a spot that wasn't numbed by the Novocain. I started screaming as loud as I could. He laughed and deadened that spot as well.

But for lunch that day I ate a double chili cheeseburger, onion rings, and fries; and when I arrived at home my wife was making burgers. Burgers twice in one day! That night when I went to bed, I remembered that I had a root canal earlier that day. I had completely forgotten about it. Dentists have told me that sometimes a root canal takes so well, and the pain was so great, that you forget you even had it because you feel so much better.

Like a Root Canal... But Better!

This chapter is going to hurt a little bit. Or maybe *quite* a bit! I'm going to be in there with a reamer, grinding on the abscessed root. Our reamer is God's Word, and the abscess is your sin. I might even work on some spots that aren't numb.

It's going to hurt. The good news is that once you get the root taken care of, you can enjoy a double chili cheeseburger.

If you've given your life to Jesus, your sin doesn't define you. In other words, you're not a hustler, a thief, or a cheater. But sin still dramatically affects your walk with God.

When I was a kid, my parents used to switch ("switch" is the Southern word for "spank") me whenever I messed up—which was often. Sometimes they told me to go to the backyard and get my own switch from a tree. That's why I hate weeping willow trees.

Horrible, huh? Sometimes I brought back a little twig and faked some tears, but my dad knew better. If I brought him a little twig, he would walk outside and get his own switch. I could hear him firing up the chain saw in the backyard, and then a few minutes later he would march into the house with the whole tree, ready to wallop me!

For most of my life, that's how I viewed God. If I messed up, I envisioned Him yelling, "Go get a switch!" So I found myself hiding—or trying to hide—my sin from God. We hide our sin by calling it an accident or a mistake or convincing ourselves it isn't a sin because everybody else is doing it.

But I was completely wrong about God's view of me and my sin.

The Parable of the Loving Father

Most people call Jesus' parable in Luke 15 the parable of the prodigal son, but I call it the parable of the loving father. To sum it up, the younger son left home and spent all of his inheritance on sinful living. Then a famine hit the land and the son had no choice but to feed pigs for a living, and he still wasn't making enough money to eat.

Sin ruins lives!

When the son "came to his senses," he realized that his dad had food to spare. Oh that we would come to our senses! The son felt so bad about his sin that he rehearsed his speech: "Father, I have sinned against heaven and against you. I am no longer worthy to be called your son; make me like one of your hired men" (Luke 15:18-19).

True repentance is the realization that you have sinned against God and other people, which causes a willingness to change. The apostle Paul said, "Godly sorrow brings repentance that leads to salvation and leaves no regret, but worldly sorrow brings death" (2 Corinthians 7:10). Godly sorrow means you realize you have sinned against God, while worldly sorrow means you're sorry you got caught. Godly sorrow brings permanent change, while worldly sorrow brings temporary change.

Stop there a second! How does this apply to us? Are we like the prodigal? Have we gotten used to sin? Let's find out by analyzing sin.

I have a broad definition of sin. Sin is wrong actions, wrong words, wrong thoughts, and the sin of omission.

Wrong Actions

Stealing

This ranks as one of the big ten (see Exodus 20:15). At what point could your actions be considered stealing? Have you ever taken even a post-it note that didn't belong to you? If so, then you've stolen.

Cheating

The late Larry Burkett said he thought the number one sin in the US is cheating on taxes. Have you ever cheated on your taxes or cheated on a test at school? In Proverbs 11:1, Solomon states, "The Lord abhors dishonest scales." The word *abhor* means "to hate or loathe." God hates cheating—and you don't ever want to do something that God hates.

Dishonoring our parents and embittering our kids

I include these two together because they address both sides of the relationship between a parent and a child. We're commanded to honor our parents, which means to respect and obey them (Ephesians 6:1-3). However, if your parents want you to sin (God forbid), then you are not responsible to honor them in that request. God issues the reverse command to parents: don't exasperate your kids (Ephesians 6:4). This means to provoke them to anger.

Extramarital sex

All forms of sex outside the marriage partnership. All forms. More about this later.

Homosexuality

In Romans 1:26-27, Paul recounts how men and women had exchanged natural relations for unnatural ones, lusting after one another. As a result, they "received in themselves the due penalty for their perversion." I love homosexuals and have led a few to Christ. Homosexuality is very similar to the sins of lust and alcoholism, which are addictions.

With God's help, just as people struggling with alcoholism can say no to drinking, people with homosexual tendencies can say no to a homosexual lifestyle.

Wrong Words

Lying

Like stealing, this is one of the big ten (see Exodus 20:16). This can be defined as knowingly deceiving someone with our words or just exaggerating when we tell a story. Every time we lie, we slap Jesus in the face.

Gossip

The literal definition of *gossip* in biblical Greek means "to whisper." Any time you criticize or demean people—and they aren't around to defend themselves—you're gossiping. Proverbs 16:28 says that "a gossip separates close friends." It also separates churches. I picked up a phrase from Robertson McQuilkin that I try to incorporate into my life: "The absent are safe with me." I don't want to talk about people when they're not around.

Cursing

James 3:10-11 says, "Out of the same mouth come praise and cursing. My brothers, this should not be. Can both fresh water and salt water flow from the same spring?" We curse because "out of the overflow of the heart the mouth speaks" (Matthew 12:34). Originally, James was referring to the act of cursing people, rather than cursing *around* people (what I call "cussing"). Nevertheless, the purpose of cursing is the same as cussing; the intent is to damage someone else's psyche.

Insults

Although it might seem harmless, "cracking" on people, "dissing" them, or "player hating" is a sin. Solomon understood the danger of insults. He said, "Like a madman shooting firebrands or deadly arrows is a man who deceives his neighbor and says, 'I was only joking!'" (Proverbs 26:18-19). Insults pierce the soul like a deadly arrow.

Complaining

When you complain, people think, *I don't need what you have. You complain just like I do.* It ruins your testimony. But when you smile and rejoice after something bad happens, it bolsters your testimony. People look at you and say to themselves, *I want that. How do you do that?* Paul wrote, "Do everything without complaining or arguing, so that you may become blameless and pure, children of God without fault in a crooked and depraved generation, in which you shine like stars in the universe as you hold out the word of life"(Philippians 2:14-16). The "word of life" is the gospel—so when we complain, we turn people away from the gospel. Know why I hate complaining? I want everyone to know Jesus personally, and complaining messes that up!

Wrong Thoughts

Pride

This is my number one most-hated sin—probably because it's also one of my biggest struggles. Pride is the attitude that says, "I have my rights. I deserve better." When those words come out of your mouth (or even appear in your thoughts), you know you've been infected by pride. This same malady infected Satan (Isaiah 14:12-15). Once one of the top angels in heaven, he thought he deserved better, so God gave him a one-way ticket out of heaven. Ever since his fall, Satan has been trying to infect us with pride. But look where it got him. What do we deserve? Well, we deserve hell; but God, in His mercy, has given us heaven.

Worry

Few men realize that worry is a sin. In my experience, women usually worry and men usually complain. We worry—just not as much as women. In Matthew 6:27, Jesus asks us, "Who of you by worrying can add a single hour to his life?" Worship and worry have a direct relationship. Like a seesaw, when our worship is up, our worry is down, and vice versa. Worship says, "God, you're in charge." Worry says, "I'm in control, and I don't know what to do about it."

Racism

Racism is the conscious or subconscious belief that one person is better than another based on the color of his skin. If you avoid people of certain nationalities or skin colors or if you tend to assume certain races will behave in a certain way, then you struggle with racism. Paul wrote, "There is neither Jew nor Greek, slave nor free, male nor female, for you are all one in Christ Jesus" (Galatians 3:28). Jesus doesn't see our job status or skin color; He sees our hearts. Allowing racism to influence your life is like not only slapping Jesus in the mouth but walking up to Satan and giving him a big hug. Satan loves it when we're divided.

Idolatry

This was rule number one of the big ten: "You shall not make for yourself an idol in the form of anything in heaven above or on the earth beneath or in the waters below" (Exodus 20:4). Think idols aren't a problem anymore? Guess again. I can tell you who your god is by looking at your calendar or your checkbook. What do you spend the most time thinking about? What do you spend the most money on? It's usually the idols in your life. Analyze it, gentlemen. Is the Lord your God or is something else your god?

Materialism

This coincides with idolatry. Jesus said, "Where your treasure is, there your heart will be also" (Matthew 6:21). We have so much stuff in this country, that if we ever lose it, we'll be broken. Notice my play on words here. Materialism makes us broke and brokenhearted at the same time! Our stuff has too often replaced Christ as the center of our lives.

Lust

This is my second most-hated sin! I hate lust! Men say, "Just because I'm on a diet doesn't mean I can't walk into a candy store and look." Really? Then read this:

 You have heard that it was said, "Do not commit adultery. " But I tell you that anyone who looks at a woman lustfully has already committed adultery with her in his heart. If your right eye causes you to sin, gouge it out and throw it away. It is better for you to lose one part of your body than for your whole body to be thrown into hell. And if your right hand causes you to sin, cut it off and throw it away. It is better for you to lose one part of your body than for your whole body to go into hell.

MATTHEW 5:27-30

Does this sound like a drastic way of dealing with sin? Jesus obviously didn't mean for us to literally cut off our hands or gouge out our eyes. Be He wants us to deal drastically with our sin!

According to Jesus' definition, how many women have you had? When are we going to get a grip on this sin? If you've looked at a woman lustfully, you've committed adultery in your heart.

OK, at what point does lust become lust?

I have a policy I call "Eyes left." A girl is running down the road, wearing virtually nothing, and your instinct—of course!—is to look. My rule is to immediately look left. If I'm driving and I hit something, it's not my fault—it's her fault. That's why I drive big trucks, because of the "Eyes left" rule. I'm kidding!

This is a very, very dreadful sin. Satan is chewing on the souls of men across the nation with this sin.

The Internet has made this problem so much worse. Many men are addicted to pornography. I don't know if it's true, but I've heard it's every man's battle. In order to guard myself from this cancer of the soul, I've set up a strong system of accountability. Most importantly, a software program runs in the background on my computer that sends an email to my accountability partners any time I check out a questionable site. I recommend x3watch or Safe Eyes, which you can purchase and download at xxxchurch.com (this website is also a great resource if you struggle with pornography).

How do you know if you're being deceived in this area? You don't. Satan is the father of deception (John 8:44), and he hates you. In their song "Slow Fade," Christian singing group Casting Crowns refers to this as "a slow fade when you give yourself away." A slow fade that ends in destruction.

I'm sick and tired of Satan winning in this area. I am tired of Christian men being sissies when it comes to dealing with this sin. I don't want Satan to win in anything we do in life—and he's winning here.

Enough is enough! Someone needs to punch Satan in the mouth by asking God to help us fight this sin!

Sin of Ignorance and/or Omission

A sin of ignorance is *sinning without knowing that you are sinning.* For example, causing someone to stumble by our actions is a sin. Romans 14:21 says, "It is better not to eat meat or drink wine or to do anything else that will cause your brother to fall." Drinking is not a sin, but if you cause someone to stumble by drinking then that becomes a sin. Or if we cause women to stumble by what we wear, then that is sin of ignorance.

A sin of omission is *sinning by not doing what you are supposed to do*. For example, not praying, not fasting, and not sharing our faith are sins of omission. All of these are taught in Scripture. In Matthew 6:5, Jesus implies that we should pray, by saying, "When you pray..." In the same way, Jesus implies that we should fast, by saying, "When you fast . . ." in Matthew 6:16. Finally, Jesus commanded us, in Matthew 28:19, to go and make disciples.

Chew on that for a while.

Enough said, right?

I told you it was going to hurt! You are likely guilty of at least some of these sins, aren't you? We certainly have gotten used to sin.

However, if I leave it right there, I would be doing you a disservice. I need to show you what God thinks about you in your sin.

God Doesn't Avoid You Because of Your Sin

Let's go back to the parable of the loving father. While the son walked slowly home with his head down, his father saw him from a distance. That means the son didn't sneak up on his dad and surprise him and then the father brought his son into the house and detoxified him before bringing him out to the public. No! The father was looking for the son the entire time he was gone. That is the heart of God toward us in our sin! Waiting, longing for us to come home.

Then the father ran to his son. Not just a little jog, but I picture a full-out sprint (maybe diving across the goal line!). He threw his arms around his son and kissed him—despite the fact that he still smelled like a pig! Then he put a ring on his finger and sandals on his feet and killed the fattened calf. Then they celebrated! Double chili cheeseburger!

God is running to you. Right now.

We need to deal drastically with sin!

A friend of mine says, "Sin will take you further than you ever intended to stray. Sin will keep you longer than you ever intended to stay. Sin will cost you more than you ever intended to pay."

Sin confuses us. It's like the man who jumped off a building to get the rush of falling. At each floor of the man's descent you could ask, "How is it going?" and he could say, "So far, so good!" Isn't that how sin deceives us?

 **TOOL BOX**

1. *Confess your sins right now.* The New Testament word for "confess" means to call your sin in the same way that God calls it. In other words, if you have trouble with lying, don't call it exaggerating. Repentance is much easier when you call it what it is: lying. Tell the Lord that you are sorry for hurting Him and others. Ask for forgiveness.

. . .

2. *Repent means to change your mind.* I have great news for you. God will help you repent. In Acts 11:18, the first Christians rejoiced that God granted repentance to the Gentiles. And then an amazing verse in 2 Timothy 2:25-26 says that the Lord's servant must gently instruct those who oppose him, "in the hope that God will grant them repentance leading them to a knowledge of the truth, and that they will come to their senses and escape from the trap of the devil, who has taken them captive to do his will."

3. *God is your power source of repentance.* We still need to take responsibility for our sin, but God has already given us the tools. Second Peter 1:3 says, "His divine power has given us everything we need for life and godliness through our knowledge of him who called us by his own glory and goodness." God has already given you everything you need to live for Him!

4. *Get accountability partners right now.*

5. *GET ACCOUNTABILITY PARTNERS RIGHT NOW.* Did I already say that? Just checking.

6. *Keep a short account of your sins.* As soon as you catch yourself in a sin, confess it to the Lord and someone else you trust.

7. Enjoy the double chili cheeseburger with Swiss cheese and mushrooms and onions and lettuce and...

CHRISTIAN MAN LAW #5

REAL CHRISTIAN MEN KNOW GOD'S WORD

LET ME BEGIN BY ADMITTING THAT I'M NOT THE SHARPEST KNIFE in the drawer. You could say I'm a few fries short of a Happy Meal. A few bricks short of a load. My SAT and ACT tests scores weren't high enough to get me into college on their own merit. Without football, no college in America would have even allowed me to drive onto their parking lot.

Growing up, the paddle and I were practically best friends because we spent so much time together. (It doesn't matter why, so stay out of it!) But a paddling I received in the sixth grade changed my attitude about studying.

Your school may have handled misfits like me differently, but my school used to give kids a good whippin' whenever they caused problems. When the teachers applied the rod to my bod, I just laughed and made fun of them—except for our assistant principal. He was a home run hitter in softball, and when he spanked me he lifted me right off the ground. I cried. (Shut up—you would have cried too!)

At that point in my academic career, D's and F's were as common as the ever-present paddle. But the day the assistant principal gave my backside a home run, another teacher witnessing the event asked me, "Why can't you get straight A's like your brother?" That made me mad, so mad that I started studying hard just to show her. From seventh grade on through high school I made a lot of A's because I studied two hours every day after football, basketball, or baseball practice.

When colleges began recruiting me to play football, the admissions director at the school I eventually attended didn't want to accept me because of my low SAT score. The football coach got a little mad and told the admissions person to look at my transcript. He was blown away when he saw that I earned a 3.85 GPA even though I took some difficult classes. When he asked me to explain the discrepancy between my grades and my test scores, I told him that I busted my tail to make good grades because I knew I wasn't as smart as other students. As a result, the college accepted me!

Incidentally, on my first day of college I gave my heart to Jesus! I look back and believe God used that paddling to inspire me to work harder in school and lead me to my particular college, where I was born again.

I taught myself how to work hard on my grades, and I transferred that work habit to reading the Bible. At times reading the Bible can be difficult, but it is worth the time and effort in the long run—like my studies were worth it for me!

Despite my academic challenges, people call me for advice. Weird, huh? Men ask me to counsel them about life. How is this possible? I think the key is found in Psalm 19:7: "The statutes of the Lord are trustworthy, making wise the simple." The Word of God makes *wise* the *simple!*

It doesn't matter if you're a straight-A student or a straight-D student. Colleges may have constructed barricades to keep you away, but the Word of God will make you wise.

The reason people consider me wise is probably due to the fact that I have read through the Bible about twenty-five times. In fact, I have memorized several books of the Bible (the short ones—like Paul's letters).

I'm not sure exactly how it happened, but the day I got saved I read the Gospel of Matthew in one sitting. I just couldn't put my Bible down. By the end of the week I had read the entire New Testament.

Jesus said, "If you hold to my teaching, you are really my disciples. Then you will know the truth, and the truth will set you free" (John 8:31-32). If you want to follow Jesus—if you want to be His disciple—then free yourself of the entanglements of this world by making the truth of God's Word a part of your everyday life. God's Word will set you free!

The longest chapter in the Bible, Psalm 119, makes some pretty bold claims about God's Word. Of the 176 verses, 172 talk directly about God's Word.

- Keeping God's Word keeps us pure (Psalm 119:9).
- God's Word gives us direction (Psalm 119:105).
- In the midst of trouble and distress, God's Word gives us delight (Psalm 119:143).

You get the point.

God gave us His Word to guard us and help us thrive. Some people view the Bible as a negative book that tells us how bad we are. Just the opposite is true! God's Word will fuel your passionate life with Christ. If you want to be a man of passion, you're going to need the Word of God to guide you.

Making Time in Your Schedule

Most Christian men believe everything I've written to this point, but then they throw their hands up in the air and say, "I don't have time to read the Bible!" Finding time in their schedule would require an act of Congress.

Men, we need to be proactive and *change* our schedule—even if it means going to Congress! Your schedule will not change itself. Conflicts are inevitable, but you can make time for the God who loves you and gave you a book that will tell you how to build a relationship with Him.

Many of us fail to make time to read the Bible because we find it difficult to understand. As much as we like to think of ourselves as challenge-oriented beings, we often shy away from anything that doesn't come naturally or we cannot comprehend. All too often, we reach for a quick fix to any problem in our lives. But if you consistently hide the Word of God in your heart, you *will* produce spiritual fruit and a mindset that guards you from stumbling blocks. But if you think reading a chapter or two from the Bible over the span of a month will change your life, you're mistaken.

That's why this is a Man Law. Are we not men? Let's be strong-minded, strong-willed, and get after it.

That said, if you miss a day, don't beat yourself up about it. Just get after it the next day. God doesn't want us moping and beating ourselves up for our failures; He wants us to respond by drawing nearer to Him again.

You've taken the time to read this book, and I'm thankful that you have. But the reality is, when you finish reading it your schedule will still remain unchanged. You need to figure out a way to get up a little earlier, go to bed a little later, or find time to read God's Word during the day.

Your Bible is like a GPS sent from God. Would you leave on a trip without a roadmap or GPS if you didn't know where you were going? Of course not. Similarly, we can't get to where God wants us to go, metaphorically, without the Bible as our guide, our spiritual roadmap.

Principles That Will Help You Read the Bible Consistently

When I was a college student, my future wife, Lisa, wrote me lots of love letters. She often soaked them in perfume overnight and then put lipstick on her lips and kissed the letter and envelope all over. Boy did that light my fire! My roommate usually picked up our mail, and when he removed the letter from the mailbox, the whole mailroom smelled like perfume— much to the envy of all the football players.

One time Lisa went overboard on the perfume. When I picked up her letter, the guys started looking around the room for some mysterious woman who had walked in. After a few seconds, they realized the strong aromatic smell was coming from my letter. "Dude, you lucky dog, who's the girl?" They were totally jealous of me.

Imagine that you're a college football player suffering through two-a-days at training camp. During training camp, we wouldn't see a girl for weeks at a time. One day you walk to your mailbox and you pull out one of those sweet-smelling letters from your girl. Cha-ching! You decide to take it back to your room and read it at your desk. But first you need to hurry to lunch, because you eat together as a team.

When you get back to your room, the whole place smells like perfume. *I can't wait to read this*, you say to yourself, *but first I need to get a power nap before I go back to practice.* You go to sleep, and when the alarm goes off you hit the snooze bar a few times; and suddenly you realize you have three minutes to get down to the practice field. *I'll read it after practice*, you promise yourself as you run out of your room. After practice, though, the guys want to hang out, which you enjoy doing anyway. Later you all go back to your room and watch a movie together. Afterward, you're too tired to read. *I'll read it in the morning*, you decide.

Three weeks later you sprain your ankle. Finally you have time to read the letter! So you hobble back to your room, pick up and the letter, and blow off the dust. That sweet perfumy smell is gone. You open the envelope and start reading. What a great letter! Your girl tells you how much she misses you and that she's praying for you. You can't believe how fortunate you are to have a girl like her. Then, at the end, you read these terrifying words:

"My birthday is in two days. I'd appreciate you calling me on that day."

Imagine what your girl would say if you did that to her.

I conducted an informal poll and asked various women what they would call someone who did that to them. One lady shouted out, "Loser!" Another one said, "Dirtbag." Another said, "Pond scum." One of them said, "*Ex*-boyfriend." That was funny. All kinds of different names.

Did you know that the Bible is a love letter from God? Jesus poured the perfume of the Holy Spirit all over it and kissed it from top to bottom with His approval. But all too often we take

His love letter home and leave it on our desk or in our bookshelf, where it gathers dust. We think our schedule leaves us no time to read it.

Ironically, when something bad happens and we end up in the hospital, the first book we open is the Bible.

What names did those women use? Loser. Dirtbag. Pond scum. Ex-boyfriend.

I sure am glad Jesus doesn't say those things to me. This leads us to our first rule about God's Word...

Rule #1:
The Bible is a love letter. Treat it that way.

Now let's move on to the next one . . .

Rule # 2:
To understand the Bible better,
you need to read it using all five senses.

Imagine taking a ball of dough and kneading it and then smashing it into a perfect circle on a wooden tray. You pour a quart of tomato sauce over it and then throw two or three pounds of cheese on top. I love cheese! Love it! Next, you layer it with pepperoni, some sausage, and some mushrooms. Then you stick it inside a wood-fired oven. Now listen to the noise of your pizza cooking. If you listen closely over the crackling wood, you can hear the crust beginning to bubble as the pepperoni begins curling up and the cheese melts. Hungry?

It's time to take it out of the oven. As you set it on the counter, you cut that delicious Italian goodness into perfect slices. They're calling your name! Ohhh, it smells sooo good. You pop open a can of your favorite soda and pick up a slice. It's so thick you've got to cut the cheese—Wait, that's the wrong phrase! How about *slice* the cheese? You fit as much of the slice into your mouth as you can, savoring every moment as it greets your tongue's taste buds.

Did you see it? Did you hear it? Did you smell it? (I know you did.) Did you touch it? Did you taste it?

See, reading is more fun when we involve our imagination. That's the way we read books when we were kids. We placed ourselves in the middle of the story.

If you read in the Bible that Jesus appeared in the Upper Room even though a door was locked, don't believe it. Examine a door. Then say to yourself, *Wait a minute, the door was locked. How'd He get in here?* He probably didn't climb outside the house to the second story—He just showed up! We don't know how, but feel that surprise and awe for yourself.

When Jesus asks the disciples in John 21:9, "Do you have any fish to eat?"—smell the fish. Say, "Wait, is that halibut? No, tilapia." Eat some fish with Him.

When you read the Bible like that, Scripture becomes real to you and it registers more easily in your long-term memory.

Rule #3:
Underline, highlight, star, add question marks.

Some people struggle getting past the fact that it's OK to write in your Bible. Your Bible is nothing more than two cows hugging a tree! It's leather and paper. The book itself isn't holy; the words are. In fact, the worse it looks, the better off you'll be. If your Bible is falling apart, your life usually isn't.

You. Are. Allowed. To. Write. In. Your. Bible. Period.

Read your Bible along with a pen that won't bleed through the page. Some people like to use highlighters. My wife's Bible has, like, fifty different colors in it. It's so stinkin' sweet.

Draw a star by a verse or underline a passage that means something to you. You can even write in the margin, explaining why that verse or passage is significant. And every time you put a star by a verse, tell someone about it that same day. Don't keep it to yourself; let it be a light to others, the same way it was to you.

In my favorite verse, Acts 20:24, Paul says, "I consider my life worth nothing to me, if only I may finish the race and complete the task the Lord Jesus has given me—the task of testifying to the gospel of God's grace."

When I first read that verse and felt God using it to bring focus to my life, I couldn't stop putting stars beside it. Star, star, star, star, star . . . I put eleven stars by it. So I told eleven people that day about that verse. And I tell someone about it every time I come across it. If I flip to that page and see it, I tell someone.

I also use question marks, which indicate questions I have about that passage. Men, it's OK if we don't have the answer to every question about Scripture. Question marks are the best way for you to grow in Christ.

Why do I say that? If you want to be discipled by someone, you need to ask questions. Otherwise, how will the person discipling you be able to identify your spiritual needs? He doesn't know what you *want* to know and what you *already* know. The best way to grow in your relationship with Christ is to ask questions. So make a notation next to your questions, then go to your pastor or Bible study leader or someone you trust who might be able to help you.

Rule #4:
The Word of God is a weapon.

I can't find many "man verses" better than Hebrews 4:12:

The word of God is living and active. Sharper than any double-edged sword, it penetrates even to dividing soul and spirit, joints and marrow; it judges the thoughts and attitudes of the heart.

Did you notice that the Word of God is described as a double-edged sword? I like double-edged swords, because they allow us to cut in both directions.

While speaking to a group of men one time, I was asked what this verse meant. So I invited a bunch of college football players to walk up to the front of the room, and then I asked them to take their fists and pound on my back as hard as they could. My mouth was taped shut, my hands were tied behind my back, and my feet were bound—all with imaginary tape or rope.

Then the center from the team ran across the room and clubbed me across my back and dislocated my shoulder. Some illustration, huh? I popped my shoulder back in. (That hurt!) Then I turned to the football players and said, "OK, that's enough, guys. It's time for me to change the rules. This time I'm going to free my mouth, my hands, and my feet."

But still, what could I do against all these big football players? I'm 6-6 and 200-something pounds. (Don't worry about the specific number!) But still, what could I do?

Then I said to everyone in the room, "Imagine that I have machine guns in both hands. Would all those guys be willing to come after me? Nothing doing. Nothing could protect them from my bullets." The point is, the Word of God is a powerful weapon to help us fight sin and assist us in our struggle against the enemy.

When Paul lists the armor of God in Ephesians 6:10-18, the Word of God is our only piece that's offensive. The rest are defensive. Maybe you could use your shield to bash someone across the head, but it's a shield for crying out loud. The sword of the Spirit—the Word of God—is an offensive tool. It's a weapon, men.

Jesus had been fasting for forty days and nights and He was hungry. I can appreciate that! But He was a lot more than hungry. After twenty-seven days of fasting, the body starts eating itself alive. You can only live on water for about forty-five days, so Jesus was literally starving to death. If Jesus ever experienced a weak moment, this was it.

Satan "happens" to show up and says to Jesus, "If you are the Son of God, tell these stones to become bread." That's quite the temptation. The enemy—and he's *your* enemy—will tempt you in your greatest weakness, where it's easiest to fall. He'll hit you there first and often.

Jesus looked at the devil and said, "Man does not live on bread alone, but on every word that comes from the mouth of God."

Bam! Now that's pretty interesting. Jesus said we live on the Word of God. He was starving to death, and with the blink of an eyelash He could have easily turned the stones into bread. But instead He said, "My food is the Word of God." Powerful.

Jesus resisted temptation by quoting a Bible verse. That's no coincidence. Even Jesus fought Satan with the double-edged sword. You can read more about it in Matthew 4:1-11.

Rule #5:
The Word of God is food for your soul.

When Jesus said He lives on every word that comes from the mouth of God, He meant it. The Word of God is food for your soul.

In Jeremiah 15:16, the prophet Jeremiah says to God, "When your words came, I ate them; they were my joy and my heart's delight." In Ezekiel 3:3, God instructed Ezekiel to eat a scroll, after which the prophet remarked, "It tasted as sweet as honey in my mouth."

You wouldn't drive across the country without a map or GPS— and you'd be foolish to start out with an empty gas tank. Every day, bring your map and fill up your tank.

Let's get on it, men!

 **TOOL BOX**

1. Spend some time chewing on 1 John 5:3: "This is love for God: to obey his commands. And his commands are not burdensome." We cannot obey God's commands if we don't know what they are. Reading the Word is directly linked to loving God.

2. People ask which translation I prefer. While I often read the New International Version (NIV), it's not necessarily my favorite. My favorite is the New American Standard Bible (NASB) because it more closely follows the Greek and Hebrew

texts. It's more accurate, but a little more difficult to understand.

3. If you don't know where to start, begin by reading the Gospel of Matthew in the New Testament. Read the Gospels (Matthew, Mark, Luke, and John) twice before going elsewhere.

4. Build a daily routine that includes spending time in God's Word. Choose a regular time in the morning, afternoon, or evening that works best for you.

5. If you need to, buy the Bible on CD and listen while you drive your car. Or buy it in a digital format and listen on your MP3 player while you exercise.

6. Bring your Bible to work or school so often that you feel naked without it.

7. If you want to go really deep in studying God's Word, sign up for an online hermeneutics class at www.ciu.edu. Hermeneutics is the study of interpreting the Bible. That class changed my study of the Word forever. I use it every day!

8. Memorize as many verses as you can. Write down a Scripture passage on an index card and then stick it in strategic places. Place it on your desk at work, on the mirror in your bathroom, or in your car so that you can glace at it while waiting at a

stoplight (Don't forget to go!). A friend of mine memorized a verse a day for a thousand days. Pick a number of days and try it.

9. You can do it!!

CHRISTIAN MAN LAW #6

REAL CHRISTIAN MEN KNOW WHAT THEY BELIEVE

IN THE MOVIE *FORCE 10 FROM NAVARONE*, TEN MILITARY specialists are assembled for an important mission during World War II. There's a demolition guy, a recon guy, a sniper . . . you get the idea. Harrison Ford plays one of the lead specialists. It doesn't get more manly than that. Throughout the movie the men wear cut-up shirts, with their muscles rippling through. It's a man movie, no question.

Their assignment is to destroy a bridge that the Germans control. When they arrive at their destination, the demolition guy decides the best strategy is to go upriver and take out the dam. So they sneak up to the dam, set the explosives, and run away as fast as they can. Of course the movie shows them running in slow motion, with the music climaxing in the background.

The bombs go off, the picture shakes, and dust covers the screen. After the air settles, the dam still remains intact. Nine of the ten guys start to panic, pacing back and forth and wondering out loud what went wrong. But the demolition guy is leaning against a tree with a piece of straw in his mouth, totally relaxed.

"Hey, why didn't it break?" they scream at him.

The man calmly looks at his watch and says, "Thirty-two more seconds." He's relaxed because he knows what's going on—*he* set the explosives.

Then, on the side of the dam, a little crack appears. Then another, and another. All of a sudden the river comes whoooshing over the crumbling dam. The water surges downstream and takes out the bridge and the Germans standing on it. The Americans win the war.

Salvation Is Often Like That Dam

Oftentimes, the bridge represents a person's salvation and the river represents the Holy Spirit. But upstream, the Holy Spirit is dammed up. The dam often represents a person's unanswered questions about God, Jesus, sin, etc. Many times people have basic questions about God that the average Christian man simply doesn't know the answers to.

We need to know those answers because people need someone to answer their questions. That way the dam will break and they can give their hearts to Jesus. But also, knowing these truths will strengthen us dramatically. When our beliefs are built on a solid foundation of truth that we can prove, we can handle any storm. Wow! Just writing that makes me feel good!

The more we know about God's truth, the more we know about God. And the more we know about God, the more we worship and enjoy Him!

If you feel a little intimidated about theology and apologetics, let me encourage you. I'm not the sharpest knife in the drawer —I'll put it that way! If I can learn this, you certainly can.

The Importance of Preparation... And Listening to God

One time on a flight I sat in first class next to a guy who was wearing what must have been a $2,500 suit. It looked waterproof; I could even see my reflection! I asked him what he did for a living and he replied that he worked for the Defense Department.

"Whoa!" I said. "If you work for the Defense Department and you wear a suit like that, you must be at a level where you aren't allowed to tell me about it. Smile if you're at that level."

He laughed and said, "You shouldn't ask me that question." I surrendered instantly.

"So what do *you* do for a living?" he asked.

I was waiting for the question. "I'm an evangelist."

"Hmmm," he grunted. "My best friend is born again."

"Why aren't you?" (Isn't that what he wanted me to say?!)

"No one can answer my questions. That's why I'm an atheist."

"Look," I told him, "we have an hour and a half. Ask away."

He began asking some very intense questions about topics that I had previously studied. I've debated some of the top evolutionists in the country and I still haven't lost a debate. Like I said, I may not be smart, but I *have* done my homework. First Peter 3:15 tells us, "Always be prepared to give an answer to everyone who asks you to give the reason for the hope that you have." So I have studied out of obedience and love!

Real men study and prepare themselves for the tough, yet basic, questions. It is a Man Law!

Finally, the man from the Defense Department asked me, "Why would God make the world look like it's billions of years old when it's not? That seems deceptive."

Wow! Great question. I had no idea how to answer that one. While I was thinking about how to respond, the plane banked, and suddenly I was looking out the window at the Louisiana bayou. It was beautiful. Then the thought hit me like a ton of bricks. God gave me the answer!

"By my definition," I responded, "to create means you give something the appearance of time. If a sculptor takes six months to sculpt a woman out of marble, it would take millions of years for it to be created accidentally. When God made this planet, He made it beautiful. It looks like it is billions of years old if you don't believe in God, but when you create something you make it look old!!"

The man threw his arms in the air and said, "You've answered all my questions!"

"Do you know what to do next?" I asked.

"I want to be born again like my best friend," he said, as he bowed his head and started to sob. "Jesus," he prayed, "I am so sorry that I have doubted you all my life. My sins are horrible and I desperately need to be forgiven. I give you everything. I want you to take over."

As he finished his prayer, the plane landed. Amazing! Go God!

As we said good-bye, he told me he was going to call his best friend.

Let's get ourselves into a knowledgeable position so God can use us!

The Basics of Defending Your Faith

I lead Q and A sessions at colleges and universities around the country—to which I encourage Christians to invite their most skeptical friends. I want people to ask questions about Christianity. This serves two purposes. First, Christians get answers to questions with which they may be wrestling. Second, skeptics get their questions answered as well. On average, 30 percent of the people in attendance have given their hearts to Christ as a result of this phenomenal ministry.

Here's the basic format I use to help people place their faith in the truth. God has worked through it to help me lead many atheists and nonbelievers to Jesus. Hopefully you'll find it helpful too.

12 o'clock: God

Sometime in the past I learned an illustration that proves our faith is rooted in the truth.

At 12 o'clock, at the top of the illustration, is "God," with an arrow pointing to 3 o'clock, where we see "Jesus." The arrow then leads to "Miracles" at 6 o'clock and then to "Bible" at 9 o'clock. Arrows also go backward and across the circle, so that the four points are interconnected.

The best place to begin your discussion is with the existence of God, at the top of the clock. Simply put, a watch proves God's existence. A tornado has never blown through a watch factory and created a watch by accident. Everyone knows that's impossible. A watch cannot exist without a watchmaker. Order does not occur on its own, because anything ordered must be created by a higher order.

12 o'clock: God

I once listened to Donald S. Coffy, a leading authority on cancer and DNA—and the Director of Research for the Brady Urological Institute of Johns Hopkins University—explain the chances that a lightning strike could create one DNA molecule in a primordial soup. He said during his seminar that the odds were about the same as if an infinite number of monkeys and an infinite number of typewriters were stuck in the same room and one monkey accidentally typed out the entire Encyclopedia Britannica series.

Then Dr. Coffy compared a giant ape to a human. He explained that the two share 95 percent of the same DNA. At that point I started to sink in my chair, thinking he was going to use this to justify the theory of evolution. But then he said, "In that 5 percent, the DNA molecules are quite different. The chances of even one DNA mutating from an ape to a man are about the same as the monkeys and typewriters creating the encyclopedia."

Next he showed everyone a slide with the Bible open to Genesis 1:1: "In the beginning God created the heavens and the earth." He said that the only explanation for DNA, scientifically speaking, is that a higher power made it. Wow! I didn't see that coming! Then he explained that God must have created the heavens and earth. Order cannot come out of disorder unless something created the order. DNA cannot exist without a DNA-maker. You cannot have an eyeball without an eyeball-maker, nor can you have an iPod without an iPod-maker.

Apologists call this "irreducible complexity."

A watch is irreducibly complex—not as complex as the human body, but if you disassemble a watch it will no longer function. Irreducible complexity means the object is complex, but it cannot be reduced and still function.

A human cell is irreducibly complex. If you remove any part of a cell (for example the Golgi body or the nucleus), it will no longer function as a cell.

One time when I was explaining irreducible complexity during a debate with a professor at a university, he dropped his shoulders and said, "You're more scientific than me!"

"Then why are you teaching this stuff?" I asked.

"I don't know," he confessed. "Maybe I should become a Christian."

God is the Higher Order who created the order!

That's 12 o'clock.

3 o'clock: Jesus

At 3 o'clock in our illustration, we see the word "Jesus." Jesus claims to be God.

We know He lived and we know He claimed to be God. We have both biblical and extrabiblical evidence. Many writers, such as Josephus and Pliny, wrote about Jesus and His followers causing great change throughout their regions. His claims form the cornerstone of Christianity.

In John 10:31-33, Jesus asked the Jewish religious leaders if they were going to stone Him because of the miracles that He had done. They answered, "We are not stoning you for any of these [miracles], but for blasphemy, because you, a mere man, claim to be God."

Based on Jesus' claims, we can offer only three explanations: He's God. He's a liar. Or He's crazy.

The insanity argument doesn't seem likely because His teachings are organized and philosophically sound—even atheists will admit this. So that leaves us with only two options: Jesus was either a liar or God.

That's 3 o'clock.

6 o'clock: Miracles

Now we come to 6 o'clock and "Miracles." If Jesus worked miracles, the liar option would be immediately eliminated, because the miracles would prove He is God.

Jesus said, "Believe me when I say that I am in the Father and the Father is in me; or at least believe on the evidence of the miracles themselves" (John 14:11). He was saying, "If you don't believe what I'm saying, at least believe what I'm doing."

How do you reproduce Jesus' miracles so that you can prove them? You can't. But you can come really, really close to proving one, based on the evidence. It still requires a little step of faith, but not a leap.

The miracle I'm referring to is the resurrection, which forms the bedrock of the Christian faith. The resurrection proves Jesus' claim of being the Messiah. If He rose from the dead, then He is who He says He is. It validates Him. Mohammad is still in the grave. So are Buddha and Joseph Smith. Follow me?

But how can we prove it? Well, all the disciples were martyred, according to tradition, while claiming Jesus rose from the dead (except Judas Iscariot, who died before Jesus). Were they telling the truth or lying? Ten of the remaining eleven were killed, partly because they refused to give up this belief. The only disciple who died of natural causes was John. According to Tertullian, the ancient church father, he was exiled to the island of Patmos after his persecutors were unsuccessful in killing him by dipping him in boiling oil. While there, John wrote the book of Revelation.

But consider the high price Jesus' disciples paid for believing in His resurrection. James was beheaded. Bartholomew was flayed alive, a form of torture where a person's skin is ripped off. Thaddeus was killed after being shot with a javelin or arrows. Matthias, who replaced Judas Iscariot, was thrown from the temple and beaten to death with clubs. As Peter was about to be hanged on a cross, he said he wasn't worthy of dying in the same manner as Jesus, so he was crucified upside-down. Matthew and Paul (who wasn't one of the original Twelve) were beheaded. The remaining five disciples were killed in various ways, as well, for claiming that Jesus rose from the dead.

This begs the question: Why would someone die a violent, torturous death for what they knew was a lie? Psychologists would tell you that this is impossible for any healthy person. Your mind wouldn't allow it to happen. Who would willingly suffer torture or be martyred for what they knew wasn't true?

The disciples never benefited financially from their beliefs—in fact, they lost nearly everything they owned. They were reviled and lived hard lives. Why would they lie to gain nothing?

Jesus rose from the dead—the greatest miracle of all—which means Christianity is true!! That is the 6 o'clock miracle.

9 o'clock: The Bible

We have now arrived at 9 o'clock, which brings us to the Bible. I never begin with questions about the Bible—I always go from 12 to 3 to 6 before proceeding to 9.

We can say with confidence that the Bible is reliable. According to the noted apologist Josh McDowell, the Bible has never been disproved by archaeology. Archaeologists often read the Bible to figure out where to dig.

For example, doubters claimed that no evidence of a man named Pilate existed outside of Scripture. However, in 1961 archaeologists unearthed a big stone slab with Pilate's name on it that coincides with the time of Jesus' crucifixion. My wife has a photo of her standing next to this slab.

Consider this: the Bible was written by 40 authors over a span of 1,500 years and it still has one theme—the reconciliation of man to God. Five authors writing about World War II wouldn't be able to accomplish this!

The Bible, 9 o'clock, also strengthens 12, 3, and 6 o'clock!

Remember that facts don't save people; God saves people. However, don't ever let that disqualify you from being used by God. Study your face off and learn as much as you can so that God can put you in situations where you can be used by Him! He wants to do it!

 **TOOL BOX**

Here are some resources that have been extremely helpful to me, but don't let the list overwhelm you. I have studied these throughout my life. Just pick one and run with it.

Books:

- *Ready Defense*, by Josh McDowell
- *More Than A Carpenter*, by Josh McDowell
- *The Case for Christ*, by Lee Strobel
- *Icons of Evolution*, by Jonathan Wells

Websites and Movies:

- www.answersingenesis.org
- www.creationingenesis.com
- www.creationscience.com

Any video or book by Bob Cornuke. Cornuke is an ex-military/SWAT commander who embarks on expeditions to locate items and locations mentioned in the Scriptures. His travels have helped him identify the real Mount Sinai, Paul's four anchors off the coast of Malta, the ark of the covenant, and more. Very interesting.

Expelled: No Intelligence Allowed. This documentary, hosted by Ben Stein, examines the issue of academic freedom in American universities and proves that there is none in the debate over intelligent design.

CHRISTIAN MAN LAW #7

REAL CHRISTIAN MEN SHARE THEIR FAITH

ONE OF MY GOALS IN LIFE IS TO BE THE ANSWER TO SOME grandmother's prayer, *Lord Jesus, please send someone to talk to my grandson about You!*

I was in an airplane waiting to depart from the terminal (pre-9/11) when a young man ran on board and sat next to me. He smelled like a cross between a brewery and a marijuana factory. Needless to say, he was drunk *and* high! His ticket was still in his hand, which meant no one from the flight crew knew he had boarded. The flight attendant didn't see him because her back was turned while she was hanging up the microphone after giving the safety instructions. Then I saw her mouth to her coworker, "Did someone just come on this flight?"

Not wanting to get the guy next to me in trouble, I kept my mouth shut. The flight attendant, however, needed to account for the additional passenger, so she walked down the aisle counting heads. Finally, she stopped beside the man sitting in front of me, who had a little boy sitting on his lap, and asked, "Sir, is your son ticketed?"

"Yes," he said. Then she mumbled something about the little boy and the extra passenger on board.

I wanted to scream, "NOOOOOOOOOO! He's sitting right next to me and he's making me high from the smell!" But I didn't say a word. I figured God was somehow involved.

So we started talking. He was really loud; and since Paul said to become all things to all men, I started talking loudly back to him, which meant that just about everyone in our area was listening to our conversation. He asked me what I do for a living, and I told him I am an evangelist. Then he yelled, "Oh my God, my grandma has been wanting me to meet someone like you!"

My new friend didn't give his heart to Christ on that flight, but I invited him to bring his live-in girlfriend to the church where I was speaking the next Sunday. When I stepped off the airplane, I assumed I would never see him again. But after the worship service the next Sunday morning, a long line of people waited to talk to me. And guess who the last two were? That's right! The young man gave me a bear hug and yelled, "You'll never believe it—this morning I gave my heart to Christ! I'm so glad we sat together on the airplane!! I can't wait to tell Grandma!!"

This story has been replayed in my life in different forms over and over as a result of the prayers of a grandparent, parent, or spouse. I want to be the answer to someone else's prayers. I want God to use me!

This is a Man Law! The time has come for Christian men to stand up and be counted! We need to share our faith in the workplace, in our neighborhoods, with our friends, etc. We need to walk through fear and man up!!

·   ·   ·

We Need to Walk the Walk *and* Talk the Talk!

St. Francis of Assisi was used by God a long time ago, but he said something that really bothers me. These words have been quoted in the church around the world for centuries: "Share the gospel at all times, and use words when necessary."

I'm diametrically opposed to that; can't get any farther away. Even as I write this it bothers me.

I understand why Francis said it. People in his day were probably talking about God but not living it out. They were talking the talk but not walking the walk. Makes sense.

Today, though, we are experiencing the exact opposite situation. Many people are trying to walk the walk—they're trying to live for Christ—but they aren't talking the talk and sharing their faith. They believe that living a Christian lifestyle is enough. Some call it "lifestyle evangelism."

Obviously, our lifestyle is very important. We'll ruin our testimony if we say one thing and live a completely different way. My point is, which wing of a bird is more important—left or right? We need both to fly. In the same way, both lifestyle and words are necessary when sharing our faith!

People use St. Francis' quote as a crutch, presuming that their actions are enough. No, it takes more than that. Without words, sharing our faith is impossible.

The apostle Paul writes:

 How, then, can they call on the one they have not believed in? And how can they believe in the one of whom they have not heard? And how can they hear without someone preaching to them? And how can they preach unless they are sent? As it is written, "How beautiful are the feet of those who bring good news!"

… Consequently, faith comes from hearing the message, and the message is heard through the word of Christ.

ROMANS 10:14-15, 17

People cannot place their faith in Jesus without someone explaining who Jesus is.

Our Biggest Problem *and* Biggest Ally

The biggest problem men face concerning this issue is fear. How do we overcome our fear?

Did you know that Paul wrestled with fear? He confessed to the Corinthian church that he came to them with fear and trembling (1 Corinthians 2:3). He also asked the church in Ephesus to pray for him to share the gospel fearlessly. He asked for it twice in fact (Ephesians 6:19-20)!

But please understand: Fear is not our enemy. Fear is our ally.

Without fear, I'd probably stick my hand in the fire more often. I'm afraid of the pain, so I don't do it.

In a way, fear helps me live courageously. Boldness is unnecessary without fear. Fear acts like a barrier, and boldness helps me break through it. Fear makes me study more, so I can share my faith with people more accurately. It forces me to pray more. Fear is my ally, not my enemy.

My enemy is shame. Again, Paul says, "I am not ashamed of the gospel, because it is the power of God for the salvation of everyone who believes" (Romans 1:16).

Shame is a different kind of fear. Shame is being afraid of what people think of you.

I remember one time when some friends and I were walking through a hotel and the guys I was with were talking about how they wanted to share their faith. Just then we passed a bar. So I said, "OK, let's walk in that bar right now and share our faith."

One of the guys walked outside to the bushes and threw up. Then he wiped his mouth off and said he was ready to go.

"What'd you do that for?" I asked him.

"I'm scared to death," the guy said.

"There's nothing wrong that," I replied. "Fear is natural."

That man walked in the bar, shared his faith, and came out walking high. Walking through your fear and sharing the gospel is an amazing feeling!

If you can't share your faith *without* fear, then share your faith *with* your fear. If fear is present, so what? Consider it your ally and share anyway.

Check out this passage in Hebrews, which, as I'll explain in greater detail later in the chapter on Sabbath rest, was written to prevent new Christians from abandoning their faith during persecution:

Do not throw away your confidence; it will be richly rewarded. You need to persevere so that when you have done the will of God, you will receive what he has promised. For in just a very little while,

> He who is coming will come and will not delay. But my righteous one will live by faith. And if he *shrinks back*, I will not be pleased with him.
>
> But we are not of those who *shrink back* and are destroyed, but of those who believe and are saved.

HEBREWS 10:35-39 (ITALICS ADDED)

Shrink back. The Greek word is only found in three places in the New Testament, including twice here in this passage. The word means to hide out of fear.

Christian men, listen up. We don't want to shrink back. If you shrink back, God says He won't be pleased with you. Point blank, God's Word says that. Well, we want to please the Lord because we are not those who shrink back and are destroyed. Why should we, when the end of the passage says that *we're* the ones who are saved?

In Acts 20:22-23, we read that Paul felt compelled by the Holy Spirit to go to Jerusalem, despite knowing that prison, hardship, and suffering were waiting for him there. Did you get that? The Spirit of God told him to go.

If you knew that prison and suffering were waiting for you, would you stop, turn around, and go the other direction?

Paul's words in verse 24 form my life verse. Oh my groceries, if we could just do verse 24 in all we do. Hang on to these words, guys:

> However, I consider my life worth nothing to me, if only I may finish the race and complete the task the Lord Jesus has given me—the task of testifying to the gospel of God's grace.

How much does your life mean to you? How focused are you on completing the task the Lord Jesus has given you?

Immediately following these words, Paul says that he's done his best to tell everyone about Christ. His hands are innocent of the blood of all men. Then he says, "I have not *hesitated* to proclaim to you the whole will of God" (Acts 20:27, italics added). The word for *hesitate* is the same word used twice in Hebrews for "shrink back." Paul didn't shrink back and hide because of fear. He had the audacity to proclaim the truth of God's Word. Isn't that amazing? That's why Paul is my hero!

Men, we need to be the kind of men who refuse to shrink back.

So how do we do it? How do we share our faith?

Share Your Faith With *and* Without Fear

On my way to a speaking engagement I boarded a little puddle-hopper, fifty-seater airplane. To my amazement, I was the only passenger. And I couldn't help but notice that the flight attendant was gorgeous.

Don't get me wrong. I'm deeply, desperately in love with my wife, Lisa. So I had no intentions of flirting with her. Her looks didn't affect me, because I love my wife.

The attendant walked up to me and said, "Sir, you're the only person with us on the flight today." And I was flying standby!

This woman scared me to death. In fact, I thought about getting off the plane because I didn't want anyone to even *think* I was flirting with her. So when she introduced herself, I resorted to an old line I use when I find myself in awkward situations like this.

"My name's Adrian, but my wife's name is Lisa. She's five-foot-four, comes up to about right here—my shoulder. She has blond hair and blue eyes. She's a righteous fox. That means she's holy and hot."

The flight attendant leaned back and said, "Wow, I've never heard any man talk about his wife like *that* before."

"Duh, look at you!" I said. "You're gorgeous. Every man's going to flirt with you." I just wanted to make sure the woman knew I wasn't intending on flirting with her.

She told me I was the nicest man she'd ever met and that I could have all the free beer and liquor I wanted. Stumbling over my words, I told her that I was a preacher. Then I asked if she would sit down across the aisle so we could talk about the Lord. "Why not?" I asked. "We've got a ninety-minute flight. Let's talk about the Lord for ninety minutes."

She agreed. The door to her heart was open, which allowed me to run through some diagnostics so that I could determine the state of her heart. Learning people's spiritual journey helps us understand how to share our faith with them so we can tailor it to their needs.

Here is a framework that will help you share your faith . . . either without fear or with fear.

Question #1:
"Do you know for sure if you're going to heaven?"

I usually begin by asking people, "Do you know for sure if you're going to heaven?"

Usually I give them three choices: "Yes," "No," or "I'm not sure." The flight attendant answered, "I'm not sure."

A quick aside: Remember to act normal and be yourself. God didn't intend for us to share our faith as if we were drones. Be excited and happy about the changes God has brought into your life. I use a lot of humor when I'm relating to people.

The gospel is communicated most effectively through relationships. Take a friend (or even a group of guys) out to lunch and pay for the meal—which gives you a better chance of leading the conversation. Incidentally, guys, don't take a female other than your wife out to lunch. That's a bad idea because it looks suspicious.

Ask them questions so they know you're interested in *their* world—and be sincerely interested. I once spent time with a CEO-type guy whose company produced gasoline out of garbage. During our conversation I asked him to show me the hydrocarbon chain that made this possible. He was blown away that I knew what a hydrocarbon chain was. That got him excited. He started writing it down, and I knew enough to be able to say, "Oh, you're missing a hydrogen there." He said, "Oh, you're right."

I used trivia to enter his world. If the guy you're talking to loves sports and you know something about sports, then talk about sports. The goal is to find out what interests them and then talk about it. Once you get people talking about themselves, most of the time they'll ask about you. Then tell them, in no uncertain terms, that you love Jesus. Find a way to fit it into the conversation.

You could say something like, "You know, I just love Jesus. I love Him so much that sometimes I think I'm going to explode." Use terms like that. Make it very obvious.

OK, back to the airplane...

Question #2:
"Why should God let you into heaven?"

The second question I usually ask people is, "If God asked you why He should let you into heaven, what would you tell Him?"

Listen carefully to their answer. If they respond with anything that doesn't indicate they have repented of their sins and surrendered their lives to Christ, then red flags should be waving in your mind. Don't make fun of them. You just need to know the spiritual condition of the people you're talking to. Knowing your audience is 90 percent of the battle when sharing your faith.

The flight attendant responded that God should let her into heaven because she's a good person. I complimented her and said that was a good thing.

Question #3:
"Would you like to know what the Bible says about becoming a Christian?"

The next question you want to ask is, "Would you like to know what the Bible says about becoming a Christian?"

The Bible serves as the authority of truth in your discussion, so you want the other person to agree on its authority (see the previous chapter, "Real Men Know Their Faith").

In answer to this question, the flight attendant said yes. From there I used a technique based on something I learned from fellow evangelist Ray Comfort. I asked her, "I know you said you're a good person—and I believe you—but have you ever lied before?"

"Yes," she admitted.

"And what do you call a person who lies?"

"A liar," she responded.

I told her I was guilty of that one too. Then I asked her, "Have you ever stolen anything?"

She said she hadn't, so I objected. "Wait a minute," I told her. "C'mon—you just called yourself a liar . . ."

She rethought and said she'd stolen something at some point in time.

"What do you call a person who steals?" I asked.

She said, "A stealer."

"Pittsburgh?" She didn't get that one, but I know you do. So I said, "You mean a thief?"

She nodded her head.

"Have you ever lusted after a guy?" I asked her next. My wife says that question was out of bounds, but I'm not so sure. I was still being appropriate, guys.

She said she had. So I told her that Jesus said, in Matthew 5:28, that if you've looked at a woman (or a guy) with lust, then you've committed adultery.

"Ma'am," I told her, "you're a lying, thieving adulterer."

But I didn't stop there. "Have you ever hated anyone before?"

She said she had. I told her that 1 John 3:15 says that "anyone who hates his brother is a murderer." "Now," I explained, "you're a lying, thieving, adulterous murderer."

The air in the cabin starting getting thick. As she looked at me her eyes began welling up with tears. That's when I dropped on her what I call the "Gospel Bomb." (Warning: you must handle this with care.)

I softened my voice and asked her, "Do you realize that any time you've committed any of those sins, you've hurt Jesus deeply?"

That's the key line. Second Corinthians 7:10 says that "godly sorrow"—being sorry for hurting God—"brings repentance that leads to salvation and leaves no regret, but worldly sorrow brings death."

I continued, "We've only gone through four of the Ten Commandments, but I'm sure we could keep going. I'm sure you've broken all ten in the last month. And every stinkin' time we do, we hurt Jesus' heart. We hurt Him."

The flight attendant began to sob. "What do I do?" she asked.

"If you're sorry, tell Him."

I don't tell people what to say when they pray the prayer of salvation. If they're not ready to give their lives to Christ, they're not ready. They know what's going on in their hearts better than we do. You can help them pray, sure. Tell them to let Jesus know they're sorry, and assure them that they can turn their lives over to His control. But make sure they use their own words.

The flight attendant bowed her head and prayed. When she finished praying and raised her head, she had a huge smile on her face. An amazing smile.

What I've shared here is a simple framework that you can use in any situation. I use it often.

The Five Pieces of Paper

I've devised another illustration that I call the "Five Pieces of Paper."

Tear a napkin or sheet of paper into five equal-sized pieces. Explain to the listener that the first piece represents your life at home. The second represents your life at work or school (or both). The third represents your social life. (People always mutter when you get to that one.) The fourth represents your hobbies, sports, interests, things like that. And the fifth represents all that's left—eating, driving, showering, sleeping.

Then ask, "In which area or areas do you have sins that you need to be forgiven of?"

Almost every time, people say their social life. That seems to be the area in which people have the most sin or at least recognize first. People who don't understand sin usually point to that one first because it's easier to identify.

Then give your listener the definition of sin. As I mentioned in chapter ??, sin is defined as wrong words, actions, or thoughts, as well as the sin of omission (not doing what you are supposed to do).

Ask them the question again: "In which area or areas do you have sins that you need to be forgiven of?" If they're close to giving their lives to Jesus, often they'll point to all five areas.

Then ask, "In what area or areas would you like to give Jesus total control?"

As they ponder your question, slip in this comment: "Oh, I forgot to tell you the rules. If you don't give Jesus all the areas, you can't give Him any. Jesus gave you everything and you should respond in like manner."

Most people agree that this point makes perfect sense. I have shared the gospel with many individuals in my life and no one has ever acted offended by my statement about giving all or nothing to Jesus.

Some people remark that they aren't ready, and that's totally fine. Thank them for being honest. God's timing is always perfect; He'll draw them in when it's time. You just planted a seed, so spiritually speaking it was a tremendous success. Remember that God doesn't hold you responsible to save anyone. Only God can do that!

Sharing the gospel with anyone should be considered a success. James F. Engel says that the average person must hear the gospel 6.7 times (I'm not sure where he got that number, but I like it!) before he or she comes to Christ. You may have just taken someone to 3.7.

If the guy you're talking to is ready to give his life to Christ, ask him to pray—giving Jesus control over his life by placing one piece of paper at a time in His hands. I usually take a bowl or a cup and say that it symbolizes Jesus' hands. I ask the person, while he places each paper in the bowl, to tell God he's sorry about his specific sins in that area. As he prays, he is literally handing over the control in all areas of his life to God. (It's a freeing idea, isn't it?)

After that, I grab all the papers in the bowl and clench them tightly in my fist. Then I tell the person to pry it open. I'm a pretty big guy, so people have a hard time getting into my hand. That's when I say, "Hey, that's *my* hand. Imagine *God's* hand. The Bible says that when we belong to Jesus, no one can snatch us out of His hand" (John 10:28-29). We belong to Him.

The two biggest deterrents to sharing our faith are fear of what people think and not knowing how to do it. We've hopefully dismantled the problem of fear and I've equipped you with two tools that you can use in any situation.

Gentlemen, we need to get out there and share our faith. I don't want to shrink back and hide because of fear. I want us to share our faith. Real Christian men share their faith.

 **TOOL BOX**

1. Spend some time praying and brainstorming about how you can share your faith using your personality type.

2. Study different methods about how to share your faith. If you aren't sure where to begin, visit a Christian bookstore and ask about books on evangelism.

3. Check out the Living Waters website: www.livingwaters.com. It offers helpful information and a variety of effective Bible tracts to purchase.

4. Sign up for a witnessing class at your church (if one is offered).

5. Ask to accompany your pastor on a pastoral call and watch how he does it.

6. Remember that you are God's instrument and that He is responsible for people's souls, not you. Just make sure that when He wants to use a specific tool, you know where to find it.

CHRISTIAN MAN LAW #8

REAL MEN SEE AND MEET NEEDS

As long as I don't hit any traffic, I should be OK, I said to myself while driving to a speaking event. Although I was running twenty minutes behind I still had enough time to pray backstage, because I knew how good the speaker is. You get what I'm saying

The heavy traffic was moving sixty miles per hour through an area of my city called "Malfunction Junction." People gave it that name because accidents and car problems take place there on a regular basis. Suddenly the entire tread from the tire of a car in front of me flew into the air and bounced off my windshield. It looked like the whole tire at first. I had tapped my brakes to avoid it, so I looked in my rearview mirror to see if my sudden reaction had caused any trouble. To my amazement, no one crashed.

When I drove by the car that lost its tread, I noticed the swerving driver was a Q-Tip (a white-haired lady). She safely reached the side, so I assumed that was the end of it. *What a relief*, I thought to myself. *At least that close call won't make me late.*

Go back and help her!

The random thought disrupted my internal conversation. I have never heard God's *audible* voice, but this was awfully loud for being silent.

This is going to make me late, but whatever you want Lord! I prayed.

I turned around at the next exit, drove past her car, and then turned around one more time. When I pulled behind her, she jumped out of her car.

"Praise Jesus! I knew He would send someone to help me!" she screamed.

"Yes, Ma'am; He sent me," I replied. While changing her tire, I explained that I was a minister. After finishing the job, we said our good-byes and then I raced down the highway in my car. I looked at my watch and realized I was going to be several minutes late.

You have her keys, the voice spoke to me a second time. I reached down and felt the lump in my pocket and turned around at the next exit. When I pulled behind her, she screamed again, "Praise Jesus! Praise Jesus! I knew He would send my keys back to me!"

My name was introduced to the crowd as I entered the auditorium, so I walked directly onto the platform. And praise the Lord, many people got right with God that night!

Christian Men See And Meet Needs

A friend once old me that interruptions *are* the ministry. What a brilliant insight. Interruptions don't hinder or help the ministry; they are the ministry! Do you really *see* the people in your spheres of influence? Do you see your waitress? The police officer directing traffic? Your employees, boss, or coworkers? Do you see your wife?

Do you see the needs of those around you, and are you willing to do something

about them? Christian men listen for God's voice—and then they see and meet needs.

A twelve-year-old girl was dying. Her father, the ruler of a synagogue, begged Jesus to come to his home and heal her. On their way to the house Jesus attracted a crowd that began smashing into Him, and as a result He could barely move.

A lady in the crowd was trying to get close to Jesus like the others. She knew Jesus could help her. Jewish law considered her unclean because she had been subject to bleeding for a long time. So every person who brushed shoulders with her that day would be considered unclean too. But she didn't care.

When the woman finally worked her way through the crowd, she came up behind Jesus and touched the hem of His robe. Instantly she was healed. Her twelve long years of defilement, depression, and separation finally came to an end.

"Who touched Me?" Jesus asked as He wheeled around. The horde surely quickly grew silent.

"Master," Peter answered, "the people are crowding and pressing against You."

"No," Jesus replied. "Someone touched Me—I felt my power go out of Me. Who touched Me?"

I believe Jesus knew exactly who touched Him and that He wanted her to come forward so everyone could see what God had done. In fact, I think He was looking right at her. When she stepped forward, Jesus told her that her faith had healed her (see Luke 8:40-48).

In the middle of a big crowd, on the way to heal a little girl, Jesus stopped—for one lady whom everyone else considered unclean. He saw needs and then met them!

Be a Sheep, Not a Goat

In Matthew 25:31-46, Jesus describes the day at the end of the age when He will separate all humanity, just like a shepherd separates the sheep from the goats. To His left, He will place the wicked. Their offense? They keep the focus of their lives clearly on themselves. They do nothing to show God's love to the people around them. Either they ignore those people or they see the needs but do nothing about them.

These people are the goats in Jesus' parable, those who will be cast "into the eternal fire prepared for the devil and his angels" (verse 41).

The righteous, on the other hand, do something about the needs that they see:

 Then the King will say to those on his right, "Come, you who are blessed by my Father; take your inheritance, the kingdom prepared for you since the creation of the world. For I was hungry and you gave me something to eat, I was thirsty and you gave me something to drink, I was a stranger and you invited me in, I needed clothes and you clothed me, I was sick and you looked after me, I was in prison and you came to visit me."

MATTHEW 25:34-36

"But when did we help You?" the righteous ask. They couldn't remember dealing with Jesus in a personal way.

Then Jesus offers these haunting words: "I tell you the truth, whatever you did for one of the least of these brothers of mine, you did for me" (verse 40).

When we give ourselves to meeting the needs of the people around us, we're really giving to Jesus.

While I was on a mission trip to El Salvador, a poor man asked me for a nickel. My interpreter told me he wanted to buy liquor with it.

"Can I buy you a loaf of bread?" I asked the man through my interpreter.

"No, I just need some money," he answered.

Nevertheless, I convinced him to walk to the bread store with me; and on our way I talked to him about Jesus. After buying the bread, we sat down outside the store and continued our discussion. Soon other people from the street gathered around to listen.

Later the interpreter asked me why I bought him a loaf of bread and then spent some time with him. I told him that what I did served as a testimony to everyone who watched.

We have been taught to love things and use people. This pervasive system of thought needs to change. Instead, we need to love people and use things.

I love, I love, I love to give to people who are in need! I mean, I love it! Giving brings me so much joy. So when I don't give, I'm robbing myself; and when I *do* give, I get so much more in return.

Real Christian Men Give

Growing up, I loved money. My parents gave me a dollar a week, which I kept in my pocket throughout the day to make sure it was still there!! I memorized the details on it. I especially loved that "new-dollar smell." On the top shelf of my closet I kept a shoebox depository with a security system. Actually, my security system consisted of two strips of tape placed on either side of the box. If anyone tampered with the box, I knew it, because it was moved outside of the tape. I loved money.

If we aren't careful, we can transfer this to our Christian life. Author and pollster George Barna reports that 88 percent of Christians do not tithe! That statistic amazes me. This may sound a little controversial, but I think tithing is minimalistic living. It is not manning up!!

Jesus said in Matthew 23:23 that tithing is just the beginning. He also expects us to meet needs through acts of mercy, justice, and faithfulness. And He also calls us to give offerings over and above our tithes. (I meant to say we *get* to give offerings as well!)

We read in Acts 4:36-37 that Barnabas sold a field and gave *all* the money to the apostles. Every penny. However, in the very next passage Ananias and Sapphira lied about giving all the money from selling a piece of property—and they both fell dead!

Does this mean that no one should be rich because all of us should give away all our money? Absolutely not.

We should make as much money as possible—but our attitude toward money may need to change. Paul emphasizes this in 1 Timothy 6:9-10:

> People who want to get rich fall into temptation and a trap and into many foolish and harmful desires that plunge men into ruin and destruction. For the love of money is a root of all kinds of evil. Some people, eager for money, have wandered from the faith and pierced themselves with many griefs.

You may look at this passage and say to yourself, *God must not want me to be rich!* But that is not the case here, since this passage says that the *love of money* is a root of all kinds of evil—not money itself. Loving money and having money are two different things.

Paul explains this a little further in the same passage:

> Command those who are rich in this present world not to be arrogant nor to put their hope in wealth, which is so uncertain, but to put their hope in God, who richly provides us with everything for our enjoyment. Command them to do good, to be rich in good deeds, and to be generous and willing to share. In this way they will lay up treasure for themselves as a firm foundation for the coming age, so that they may take hold of the life that is truly life.
>
> 1 TIMOTHY 6:17-19

Paul didn't say, "Don't be wealthy." He said, "Don't put your hope in wealth." So, you see, it's OK to be rich as long as we're generous. As far as I'm concerned, make as much money as you possibly can, then do good with it—be rich in good deeds, be generous, and be willing to share it. Jesus said, "It is more blessed to give than to receive" (Acts 20:35).

John Wesley said it this way: "*Make all you can*, save *all you can*, give *all you can.*"

Give and Then Trust God

One time, while I was in the process of memorizing 1 John, I woke up sobbing in the middle of the night. First John 3:16-17 was flooding through my head:

This is how we know what love is: Jesus Christ laid down his life for us. And we ought to lay down our lives for our brothers. If anyone has material possessions and sees his brother in need but has no pity on him, how can the love of God be in him?

Despite reading that verse at least a hundred times throughout my life, I had never truly grasped it until then. My mind drifted to the many people standing at intersections and holding signs that say "Will work for food" and to the homeless men and women sitting beside the buildings downtown. I thought about the starving children overseas and felt overwhelmed.

After researching different ministries that help the poor, I discovered Compassion International and jumped in headfirst. I recruited the University of South Carolina football team to sponsor twenty-five kids in the Dominican Republic. My wife and I sponsor three kids, and a Bible study I lead sponsors three more.

Compassion not only helps the kids financially; they also assist in their education and introduce them to the gospel. My youngest son—who was six years old at the time—ran through our house screaming when he learned that our sponsored child "got saved." When I asked him if he knew what that meant, he said, "No. But it *is* awesome, right?" I agreed, and he continued running and screaming! What can I pay pay to have my kids experience something like that? It's priceless!

When America's economy goes south, the world's economy—especially places like El Salvador—goes south along with it. We need to open our eyes and do something about it. People close by us also live in extreme poverty. We need to do something about that too.

We so easily make excuses for our lack of generosity. We rationalize that people are poor because they're lazy or that the homeless person asking us for money is just going to spend the money on alcohol. Jesus didn't offer any caveats on being generous. He said very clearly, "Give to the one who asks you" (Matthew 5:42).

If you're suspicious about how people will spend the money you give them, just outsmart them. Take them to a restaurant and buy them something to eat. Sometimes the greatest gift is your time and inconvenience.

If you don't have time to buy them something to eat, give them some money and say, "I wish you wouldn't use this to buy liquor. I'm giving this to you because I'm deeply in love with Jesus Christ. He's by far the greatest thing that's ever happened to me. I want to give this to you as if I'm giving it to Him."

Then trust God.

Some think that people on the street corners are running a scam. But that's not how I see it. Those men and women work pretty hard. I wouldn't sit in the cold and hold a sign. That's work to me. Those people are working their corner.

Men, we need to be aware of what's going on around us—in our communities and around the world. Then we should do something about it.

TOOL BOX

Here are some ways to do something
about the need around you:

1. Sponsor a child through Compassion International (www.compassion.com). They're like a children's ministry on steroids. They tutor needy children after school through local churches, as well as provide them with job training so they will one day be able to support their families. Through this ministry I've met impoverished kids full of the joy of Christ. In 2009 alone, 110,000 conversions worldwide were reported through their ministry.

On a recent Compassion International overseas trip I heard a young man in El Salvador say, "I live in poverty. But poverty doesn't live in me anymore." Your gifts help replace the poverty in a kid with the gospel.

2. Volunteer in your community and church to help the needy around you.

3. Give money to the homeless.

CHRISTIAN MAN LAW #9

REAL CHRISTIAN MEN ARE MEN OF PRAYER

WHAT'S THE KEY TO WINNING A WAR?

I've asked numerous generals, colonels, majors, and other military officers this question, and they all answer without hesitation: cut off the enemy's communications. When you cut off communication, you cut off the enemy's eyes and ears.

The first target in Operation Desert Storm (the Persian Gulf War against Iraq in 1990–1991), was the communications tower. Six months after the war ended, a general from the Iraqi army confessed to *USA Today* that their military had no idea what was going on at any point in the conflict!

That, men, is exactly what Satan wants to do in our lives. He wants to cut off our communication. He wants us blind and deaf to the heart of God. Prayer is our communication line to God.

Don't Be Like "The Silent One"

An ancient Jewish legend tells about a man named "The Silent One." He was given the name because he responded to adversity with patience and loving silence. He forgave quickly and always sought to do the will of God. Because of his faithfulness, the Lord sent word to The Silent One that he could have anything he wanted in all the world.

While heaven waited with baited breath, The Silent One thought long and hard. Then he responded to God's offer: "For the rest of eternity, I would like to eat hot rolls with butter every morning."

All of heaven wept.

Far too often our prayers are no different than The Silent One's. At our disposal lies an opportunity to touch the throne room of the king of the universe, to witness amazing acts that only the King of kings can accomplish. And yet our only request is hot rolls and butter, items that directly influence our personal comfort?!

We all need to pray—but in ways that line up with the heart of God.

I'll be honest. I find prayer difficult because I struggle with distractions. I just find it hard to focus on anything for a long (or short) period of time. You'd think I have ADHD-Q2Z516 set hut! (That's a joke... relax!)

Praying in the Closet

Part of the reason men struggle with prayer is that they don't know how to do it. Prayer can be broken into two categories.

I call the first type "closet prayer time." That doesn't mean you need to pray in a closet; it means you need to pray by yourself. No one even needs to know what you're doing (see Matthew 6:5-6).

Over the years I've developed a personal prayer journal to help me stay focused during my "closet prayer time." I pray according to the diagram below:

Circle #1: Praising God

Giving praise to God forms the outer circle of prayer. Praise gives us perspective and acknowledges God's rightful place in the universe and in our lives. Different names in reference to God are used throughout the Bible. We need to know these names because each of them describes a unique facet of His character.

Let's go through the names:

Elohim = Creator God (Genesis 1:1)

Yahweh (This Hebrew word is translated *Lord*) = Self-existent God (Genesis 2:4)

El-Elyon = God Most High (Genesis 14:20)

El-Roi = The God who sees (Genesis 16:13)

El-Shaddai = God Almighty (Genesis 17:1)

Adonai = Lord (Genesis 18:27)

El-Olam = Eternal God (Genesis 21:33)

Jehovah-Jireh (Jehovah is the same Hebrew word as *Yahweh*) = The Lord is my provider (Genesis 22:14)

Jehovah-Rophe = The Lord is my healer (Exodus 15:26)

Jehovah-Nissi = The Lord is my banner (Exodus 17:15)

Jehovah-M'Kaddesh = The Lord who makes me holy (Leviticus 20:7-8)

Jehovah-Shalom = The Lord is my peace (Judges 6:24)

Jehovah-Raah = The Lord is my shepherd (Psalm 23:1)

Jehovah-Sabaoth = The Lord of hosts (Isaiah 1:24)

Jehovah-Tsidkenu = The Lord is my righteousness (Jeremiah 23:6)

Jehovah-Shammah = The Lord who is there for me (Ezekiel 48:35)

Lord (Greek) = Supreme Ruler (Revelation 17:14)

Savior = The God who saves me (Luke 2:11)

Messiah = The Anointed One (John 1:41)

By learning the different names of God and then praying them, you naturally grow deeper in your relationship with God.

Here are a couple of examples of how I pray the names of God:

> 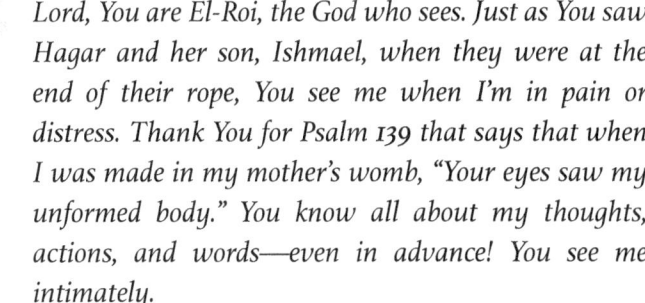 *Lord, You are El-Roi, the God who sees. Just as You saw Hagar and her son, Ishmael, when they were at the end of their rope, You see me when I'm in pain or distress. Thank You for Psalm 139 that says that when I was made in my mother's womb, "Your eyes saw my unformed body." You know all about my thoughts, actions, and words—even in advance! You see me intimately.*

> *Lord, You are Jehovah-Nissi, my banner. Just as You gave strength to the Israelite army when they fought the Amalekites in Exodus 17, so I'm confident that You will provide strength for me when I encounter a trial and look to You!*

I also pray using Scripture. A few passages to get you started include Psalm 67, Philippians 2:5-11, and Colossians 1:15-20.

This may sound a little weird, but I even like to pray back the words of songs to God. One of my favorites is Kim Walker's song, "How He Loves."

Circle #2: Missions and Ministries

After praising God, next I pray for missionaries, ministry leaders, pastors, and people I know in full- and part-time ministry in the United States, again praying for them individually by name.

Circle #3: Federal and State Officials

The Bible says to pray for your leaders (1 Timothy 2:1-4), so after that I pray for the president, other federal officials, and the government in my state, which happens to be South Carolina.

Circle #4: Friends and Family

Then I pray for my friends, followed by my family members. Do you see the circles getting smaller?

Circle #5: Supplication

Gale Sayers, the NFL Hall of Fame running back, said in regard to his priorities: "The Lord is first, my family and friends are second, and I am third." He later wrote an autobiography entitled *I Am Third*.

I pray for myself last. Bringing our requests to God is called supplication.

Did you ever own one of those Radio Flyer wagons? If you weren't carrying anything in it, the wagon rattled. But if it was full, it didn't make a sound. Most people bring God a full wagon, full of requests. But, you know, sometimes it's nice just to walk up to God's throne with an empty wagon and tell God how much you love Him. Let him hear the empty wagon rattling.

I once heard someone say, "When men work, men work. But when men pray, God works." We can work and get a lot of stuff done and even feel good about ourselves. When God works, however, He can accomplish so much more. What a rush it is to see God answer a specific prayer as only He can!

All of these concentric circles help us abide in the vine of Christ. (You can read more about that in John 15.)

Praying without Ceasing

Praying in the closet is the first type of prayer, but now I'm going to share with you another kind. I call this the 1 Thessalonians 5:17 prayer. There Paul tells us to "pray without ceasing" (NASB). Many theologians describe this as an attitude of prayer, but I think it surpasses an attitude. The passage doesn't say "have an attitude"; it says "pray."

So how do we pray without ceasing? Greek scholars Henry Liddell and Robert Scott remarked that "without ceasing" is akin to having a chronic cough. You can pray without ceasing by giving yourself little prayer reminders that jolt you into prayer throughout your day.

Here are a few ideas to help you. Some will work for you and some won't. Avoid trying to do all of them at once—just pick one or two and then add to them as you grow in prayer.

The Prayer Cup

Write someone's name in the bottom of a cheap plastic cup, the kind you buy at ballgames. Then every time you drink out of the cup, pray for that person. You don't need to offer an elaborate prayer. Just pray that the person would love God more today than yesterday, or that God would protect the person from the enemy, or something like that.

One time a friend of mine from Alaska gave me a cheap plastic cup, the kind you buy at ballgames. So I wrote his name in the bottom to remind myself of him. While drinking from the cup one day, I felt very strongly that I needed to pray harder for him. So I knelt beside my bed and prayed.

After that I walked downstairs and turned on the television to discover that the American military "accidentally" bombed the Chinese embassy in Belgrade, Yugoslavia. Violent demonstrations were taking place in China, with some Americans being beaten. The friend I was praying for was living in China at the time. In fact, demonstrations were taking place in front of his house! At the same moment I was praying for him, he walked right through the middle of the angry crowd without anyone laying a finger on him.

Did my prayer prevent him from being beaten? I don't know; and I don't care because I don't want to take credit for what God did. All I know is that the cup reminded me to pray and the Holy Spirit impressed me to pray even harder. I need all the prayer reminders I can get.

WBIP

WBIP stands for "Watch beeps, I pray." Every time I hear a watch beep—BAM!—I offer a quick prayer. It doesn't need to be long or drawn-out. Just pray for whatever is on your heart at that moment.

By the way, guys, don't be afraid to talk normal when you pray. Pray like you're talking to a friend.

Also, when you pray you don't need to thank God a bunch of times and call that a prayer. If someone walked up to you and started rambling, "I wanna thank you for this, I wanna thank you for that, I wanna thank you for that, too," you'd probably think the person was some kind of weirdo. Obviously, thanking God is good; but pray in a way that's conversational and echoes your heart and mind. Use real language. Engage your mind.

Laugh with God. He's your friend and your Father, so develop a real relationship with Him. You can even pray with your eyes open—especially when you're driving. I don't believe in blind faith!

If you pray the same prayer over and over to God, repeating what you've heard others pray, you're just being rude. Pray like you're having a conversation with God (which you are), and speak from your heart.

BRIP

BRIP stands for "Bell rings, I pray" or "Buzzer rings, I pray." If you're in school or at work and the school bell or your phone rings, pray. Offer up a quick prayer; you don't need to stop what you're doing. Like I said before, you don't even need to close your eyes. Just send your thought toward God in that moment.

Siren

Whenever you hear the siren on a fire truck, ambulance, or police car, pray for the person who's in trouble.

Shoes

Shoes? Yes, shoes. One time a kid asked me to autograph his tennis shoe. He slipped the shoe off his foot, stuck in my face, and told me my autograph would remind him to pray for me every time he put on his shoes. *What a GREAT idea*! I thought to myself, as I signed the boy's shoe as legibly as I could.

If you have expensive designer shoes or tennis shoes and you don't want to mess them up, fine. Write the person's name on the inside of the shoe, perhaps under the tongue, where you'll see it when you put it on.

Hats

This works the same way as shoes. Write someone's name on the inside of a baseball cap. Then pray for the person when you see it or wear it.

BCIB

BCIB stands for "Business card in Bible." This is a fun one. Whenever someone gives me a business card, I put it in my Bible. Then when I'm looking through my Bible and I "stumble" across the person's card (which is really God's providence), I pray for that person on the spot.

Dot on Watch

No, not Department of Transportation! I'm referring to a little dot that you can place in the middle of your watch. Let the dot represent a friend who needs Christ. Then pray for the person whenever you look at your watch.

For thirteen years the dot on my watch represented a friend who didn't know Christ. Then one day he called me and said, "Hey, AD. I got saved!"

I jumped for joy. Thirteen years of prayer—what a rush! That guy went on to become a champion for Christ, starting a Bible study that was attended by some big-time athletes in Ohio. He has led some pretty important people to Jesus.

Fuzzy Dice

The last prayer reminder I will offer you are fuzzy dice. Even if you weren't around in the 1970s, you likely remember the fuzzy dice that people used to hang from the rear-view mirror inside their car. No one has those anymore, so I'm not referring literally to fuzzy dice. I'm talking about anything you hang from your rear-view mirror. Hang something that inspires you to pray.

Ideas for prayer reminders are limitless, so develop some of your own. These are just some suggestions, little devices that have helped me to pray without ceasing, as Paul instructs us.

So let's get after it, men. We're in a war here. Satan is trying to knock out your communication tower. Are you going to allow him to do it? By staying in touch with Central Intelligence, we *will* win the battle. Let's win this war!

 **TOOL BOX**

1. Buy a journal or notebook and begin your own personal prayer journal. Leave space to note the answers to your prayers over time.

2. Chose one or two of the prayer reminders mentioned above and put them into practice.

3. Never be afraid to say the blessing at a business lunch or dinner. It will set the tone for potential conversations about God. Paul said the blessing over everyone's food after they hadn't eaten for fourteen days because a storm was threatening their ship (Acts 27:35).

4. Write down the names of five men you would like to see come to Christ. Pray for a strategy to share the gospel with them.

5. Pray!

CHRISTIAN MAN LAW #10

REAL CHRISTIAN MEN FORGIVE EARLY AND OFTEN

I WAS STANDING ON THE SIDELINE, MINDING MY OWN BUSINESS while watching my University of South Carolina Gamecocks play against our archrivals, the Clemson University Tigers. As the chaplain of the football team, my job during games is to provide support and encouragement to the team.

After our offense failed to convert a fourth down, a Clemson player got into a scuffle with one of our players, which soon erupted into a bench-clearing brawl on both sides.

Immediately, I ran onto the field to help break up the fight. With players on both sides swinging their helmets, I felt incredibly vulnerable. The police and security jumped in, trying to separate the players; but because they abandoned their posts, no one was preventing the fans from rushing the field.

The fight spread into the end zone, where I was trying to separate two players. I reminded myself to stay aware of what was going on around me because I was one of the few older adults in the area. Suddenly someone punched me in the back. I turned around and faced a Clemson player.

"I'm the *chaplain!*" I yelled at him.

A look of terror instantly came across his face. He turned around and ran down the sideline.

"Watch out for lightning!" I screamed.

Ten yards away from me, fans began surging the field. Since we were the visiting team, our lives were in danger. *God, please keep them at bay*, I prayed.

Eventually the brawl subsided and the game continued, but the experience broke my heart and threw me into a three-month depression.

Has Anyone Swung a Helmet at You?

Maybe you haven't stood in the middle of a football field surrounded by guys swinging their helmets and their fists, but I'm sure you've felt like it. Perhaps someone nailed you on the side of the head with an unfair criticism. Or someone punched you in the chest by insulting you in front of your friends. Or a friend speared you in the back by spreading a rumor about you.

Have you ever been offended?

When I was a kid, my friends used to call me names because I was tall, skinny, and had curly hair. "Lanky," "Garden hose," "Blade," and "Mop" were just a few of the names they gave me. I laughed on the outside and wept on the inside. Then, alone in my bedroom, I'd shut the door weep on the outside too.

All around us, people take sides and swing their helmets at the opposition:

- Yankees and Southerners—Where I live, some people think the Civil War is still being fought.

- Blacks and Whites—Again, in the South this is still a challenge. A white girl hugging an African-American guy started a race riot at my high school. The police were called to break it up.

- Democrats and Republicans—Every two years the fight continues where it left off at the last election.

What do you do when someone hurts *you*? What do you do when a driver cuts *you* off? How do you respond when a pastor offends *you*? Do certain types of people make you mad? Maybe you don't like lazy people. So many offenses and so little time.

This chapter is for everyone—including you and me.

Men, this is definitely a Christian Man Law, because Christian men forgive early and often!

The Story Behind the Story of the Good Samaritan

We read in Luke 10 that an expert in the law (a Bible scholar) asked Jesus, "What do I need to do to go to heaven?"

Jesus turned the question around and asked him, "You know the law. What does it say?"

"Love God with all your heart, soul, strength, and mind . . . and love your neighbor as yourself," he answered.

"That's right," Jesus told him. "Live like that and you will have eternal life."

But the lawyer wasn't satisfied with Jesus' answer. He wanted to justify himself, so, like any good lawyer, he asked a follow-up question: "And who is my neighbor?"

Jesus then gave him (and us) a parable.

A Jewish man was mugged, beaten, and left for dead. A couple of religious leaders walked by, but they didn't stop to help because they didn't want to be bothered by the interruption. Plus, if the man died they would be considered unclean, which would be a big hassle to fix.

But then Jesus said a Samaritan man walked by and stopped to care for the victim. He placed the man on his own donkey and brought him to an inn where he could recover. And before leaving, the good Samaritan paid for the man's expenses and pledged to refund the innkeeper for any additional costs that might occur in the future.

Stop for a moment to feel the tension rising among Jesus' listeners. You need to understand the revulsion Jews felt toward Samaritans. You see, seven hundred years earlier the Assyrians conquered the northern tribes of Israel. Many of the Israelites were taken captive to Assyria, and many Gentiles were brought into the land by the Assyrians. The capital of the northern kingdom was Samaria, and the entire territory of the northern tribes had come to be known as Samaria. The mixed-blood race resulting from the intermarriage of these two groups became known as "Samaritans." The Jews viewed them like half-breed dogs!

Painting a positive picture of a Samaritan in the presence of a Jew was like bragging about the University of South Carolina Gamecocks at Clemson University, our cross-state rivals! Watch out for flying helmets!

One time I picked up a plastic bottle off the football field and threw it in the trash. A football player called me "a good Samaritan." "Do you know what a good Samaritan is?" I asked him.

"Somebody who does good things for people," he replied.

Imagine that! Two thousand years later Samaritans aren't seen as half-breed dogs but rather as good, wholesome people whom you want your kids to imitate.

So what does this have to do with forgiving people who have wronged you?

People easily forget that not long before this Jesus and His disciples had passed through Samaria and had planned to stop for the night in a certain village. But the Samaritans hated the Jews so much that when the villagers learned that Jesus and His disciples were on their way toward Jerusalem, they refused to let them spend the night. James and John then asked if they should call down fire from heaven to destroy the villagers, but Jesus rebuked them and led them down the road to another village (see Luke 9:51-56).

Think about it: Jesus refused to carry a grudge. You would expect Him to be mad a few days after that, but instead He told a story that made the Samaritans look good—and two thousand years later they still look good!

Jesus refused to carry a grudge!

After speaking the parable, Jesus asked the lawyer, "Which of the three men was a good neighbor to the man who was beaten?"

The man responded, "The one who had mercy on him." The expert in the law couldn't even bring himself to say the word *Samaritan*.

Say No to the Bait

How do you forgive when someone hurts you deeply?

In his book *The Bait of Satan*, John Bevere compares unforgiveness with bait used to trap wild animals. In the same way, Satan uses offenses to bait and ultimately trap us in unforgiveness and bitterness.

Bevere describes the five-step process the enemy uses to bait us:

> 1. *After someone has hurt or wronged us, we usually respond with anger.* While short-term anger is OK, we shouldn't let the sun set while we're still fuming. Ephesians 4:26 says, "'In your anger do not sin': Do not let the sun go down while you are still angry." Jesus certainly felt angry when He drove the money changers out of the temple with a whip (John 2:15), but He never sinned. If your anger continues for more than twenty-four hours it turns into sin, because you've let the sun go down on it—which leads to the next step...

> 2. *Anger over time turns into resentment.* Resentment makes you critical. Resentful people are critical people. When you resent someone, in your opinion that person can do nothing right. A glance is a glare, and even a kind word always carries an underlying message. If, in your opinion, a person who has hurt you has few if any redeeming qualities, you have a critical spirit. In the same way, if a woman driver cuts you off, do you lump all women drivers into the same category? We have a tendency to lump all the types of people who hurt us into one lump sum. If a pastor offends us, then we have trouble trusting pastors. If a Republican or Democrat does something that disappoints or frustrates us, then

we don't trust any of them. If a woman hurts you, then you have trouble trusting women. You have a critical spirit.

3. Resentment leads to bitterness. Bitterness is resentment turned inward. Hebrews 12:15 tells us, "See to it that . . . no bitter root grows up to cause trouble *and defile many*" (italics added). Bitterness has a tendency to affect even our good relationships, because a bitter root affects every leaf of our lifestyle.

Let's analyze this for a moment. Regardless of whether or not you were at fault for the offense, if you take a bite from Satan's bait and follow the first three stages, then you have sinned three times—through prolonged anger, resentment, and bitterness. Remember that the offender may have only sinned once against you. Satan wins when sin wins. Now you see why Satan's bait is so deadly.

4. Bitterness then gives way to self-pity. Self-pity means we feel sorry for ourselves and we wonder if we are responsible for the offense. Self-pity is a significant challenge for me, and I can say from experience that self-pity stirs up feelings of loneliness and often causes people to beat themselves up.

5. Last of all, self-pity gives rise to depression. This certainly isn't the only reason people get depressed, but it is definitely one of them!! I know a man who was greatly offended and tasted depression for many months. He called it the dark side of his soul.

The Only Way to Free Yourself from the Bait of Satan

If the bait of Satan has entrapped you, the only one way to cut the line and free yourself is to forgive the person who offended you.

Peter asked Jesus, "How many times shall I forgive my brother when he sins against me? Up to seven times?" (Matthew 18:21).

Peter asked an interesting question, since the Hebrew Old Testament never says how many times a person should forgive. The rabbis in Jesus' day taught that people should forgive up to three times when someone sinned against them. The other disciples probably gasped when they heard Peter say up to seven times! They probably thought to themselves, *Wow! That Peter is a real man of God!*

But Jesus far surpassed Peter's question. He responded by saying, "I do not say to you, up to seven times, but up to seventy times seven" (Matthew 18:22, NASB). For all you remedial math students, 70 times 7 equals 490. So after the person has offended you 491 times, you no longer need to forgive—Just kidding!

Then Jesus told a parable about a king who gathered his servants to settle accounts. One owed him $15.3 billion. You may wonder how I formulated that number. The passage says that the first servant owed the king 10,000 talents. A gold talent weighed 75 pounds, so 10,000 gold talents weighs 750,000 pounds. One pound of gold is equivalent to 14.58 troy ounces, so when you multiply 750,000 pounds times 14.58 you get about 11 million troy ounces. The price of gold in the US at the time of this writing is $1395 per ounce. So multiply 11 million times $1395 and you get about $15.3 billion. Imagine owing someone that much money!

The king ordered the entire family to be sold into slavery to repay the debt. Distraught, the servant fell to his knees and begged for more time. The master then magnanimously forgave the entire debt. Wow!

Immediately after leaving the king's presence the servant found another servant who owed him about $17,500. The Scripture passage says the second servant owed the first servant 100 denarii. A denarius was equivalent to one day's wage. According to the most recent studies, the average American makes $43,362 a year. Assuming a person works 50 weeks a year, then 50 times 5 days of work per week equals 250 days. Divide $43,362 by 250 and you get an average wage of about $175 a day. Multiply that by 100 and you get the $17,500 that the second servant owed the first servant.

So the first servant, who was forgiven $15.3 billion, choked the man who owed him $17,500 and demanded to be repaid. Since the second servant didn't have the money, the first servant had him thrown into prison.

When the master discovered what happened, he reinstated the wicked servant's debt and threw him in prison to be tortured until he paid back everything he owed!

Then Jesus concludes the parable by saying, "This is how my heavenly Father will treat each of you unless you forgive your brother from your heart" (Matthew 18:35).

Wow!

If you have been born again, then God has forgiven you $15.3 billion. Obviously, I'm not referring to a specific amount of money. You have been forgiven more than you'll ever be able to repay in your lifetime. In comparison to the debt that you've been forgiven, the worst offense anyone could ever commit against you will never exceed $17,500. But let's be honest: most everyday offenses aren't worth more than $500 on that scale.

How could you not forgive someone of so much less when God has forgiven you of so much more—$15.3 billion?

Saying No to the Poison

Carrying a grudge is like drinking poison and then waiting for the person who hurt you to die. The poison kills *you!*

One day when I was in college a buddy grabbed me by my curly hair and smashed my head into a cinderblock wall for something I didn't do. I was the president of the local Fellowship of Christian Athletes (FCA) chapter and he led another ministry on campus. I could have retaliated and crushed the guy, but instead I walked away. But after that incident I despised him and his ministry. I was drinking the poison, and waiting for him to die.

About six months later someone randomly asked me if I was angry at someone. Not sure how the person would have known that!

I responded, "What do you mean? I'm the president of FCA. Don't you see my halo?"

God immediately interrupted me. *What about Mark?* He spoke to my heart. I went to my dorm room and hit my knees on the concrete floor for an hour. I figured out what forgiveness is.

You can say no to the poison too. Here's how:

> 1. Understand that the saying "Forgive and forget" is
> from Shakespeare, not Scripture. Some events that
> occur in our lives will never be forgotten. But, also, we

cannot forgive what we cannot remember. In fact, forgiveness is only understood and appreciated in the context of before and after. So after you forgive someone, that doesn't mean you should no longer remember it.

2. Remember the many ways God has forgiven you. Paul instructed his readers to "Forgive as the Lord forgave you" (Colossians 3:13). Remembering how we've offended God (and others) brings perspective on the offenses committed against us.

3. Release the offender into God's hands. If someone harms my wife, he should go to prison. Forgiveness and justice go hand in hand. But I still need to release him from the offense. You see, forgiveness isn't between you and the other person; forgiveness is between you and God. So let God take responsibility for dealing with the offender. It's no longer your problem.

4. Pray for the person who hurt you. Jesus said, "Bless those who curse you, pray for those who mistreat you" (Luke 6:28). Praying for our offenders pulls the thorn out of our heart, gives us God's perspective on the other person, and empowers the Holy Spirit to soften the offender's heart. When you pray blessings on someone who hurt you, you have come to the place of complete forgiveness!

Forgiveness is a lifelong process. Just because you forgave someone yesterday doesn't mean you won't struggle with forgiving the same offense today. Here are some ideas that will help you continue living in an attitude of forgiveness:

1. If you're driving down the road and unforgiveness starts welling up inside—the offense begins growing bigger and bigger and you grip the steering wheel tighter and tighter—hold your hand up high and say, "No! I forgave him!" Say it out loud so you can hear it and remind yourself.

2. When other people start telling stories about how they've been wronged, the temptation is to say, "Yeah, the same thing happened to me..." Don't pile on. Refuse to join in. You'll only feed the negative feelings that will give new life to the forgiven offense. Don't talk about the offense apart from a counseling situation.

3. This is the hardest one. If the offending person does the same thing to you again, treat it as if it's a brand-new offense. You've likely heard the expression, "The straw that breaks the camel's back." How in the world could a straw break a camel's back? Actually, a straw can't break a camel's back—but the weight of two million other straws can. When you forgive someone, you remove the other straws from your back so that the next straw feels like only one straw.

Forgiveness doesn't mean you should allow the person to continue hurting you. After a second offense, you should take measures to prevent the offense from happening in the future so you won't be hurt again.

Forgiveness is an act of the will, which is why this is a Man Law. Forgiveness is not for wimps; only tough men can do this!!

TOOL BOX

I. Take some time to think about someone who has hurt you deeply. Have you forgiven that person? Ask God to give you the strength to forgive.

2. After you have forgiven the person, don't walk up to him and say, "I forgave you." That accomplishes nothing. Instead, ask him to forgive you for your anger, resentment, and bitterness.

3. In his book, *The Art Of Forgiving*, author Lewis Smedes once wrote, "When we forgive, we set a prisoner free and discover that the prisoner set free is us." Unlock the key to your prison and open the door.

CHRISTIAN MAN LAW #11

REAL CHRISTIAN MEN LOVE THEIR WIVES

Nearly every time I speak, I begin with these words:

> My name is Adrian, but my wife's name is Lisa. She comes up to about right here (I point to my shoulder). Listen, guys. She is a righteous fox. That means she's holy and hot. Cha-ching!

Then I usually ask all the married men in the room to stand. I do this even if I'm speaking to a college group and I know that only a couple of married guys are sitting in the audience. While the men are standing, I tell them to yell as loud as they can why they love their wives. And I tell the men to yell LOUD.

I want everyone to hear and see the men brag on their wives.

Why do you think I do that? For some laughs? Well, maybe a little, to loosen up the room a bit. But mostly I do it because I LOVE MY WIFE! I LOVE LISA!! There's not a single thing wrong with loving your wife, or showing other people around you—even if they're strangers—that you love your wife. As a matter of fact, I think men are sissies if they don't brag about their wives.

Loving Our Wives Is a Matter of Show and Tell

Let me ask you a controversial question: Should husbands submit to their wives?

Many men have memorized Ephesians 5:22: "Wives, submit to your husbands as to the Lord." If we could, most of us would add an exclamation point to the end of the sentence: "Wives, submit to your husbands as to the Lord!"

Most people overlook the fact that the preceding verse belongs in the same section of Scripture, because most translations have added a heading in between them. Actually, the section from Ephesians 5:21 to 6:9 should be entitled "The Need to Submit to One Another."

Here's how the passage looks without a heading to separate the two verses:

> [21] Submit to one another out of reverence for Christ.
> [22] Wives, submit to your husbands as to the Lord.

In answer to the question, Should husbands submit to their wives?—Yes, men should submit to their wives, as we can see in verse 21.

However, the man's job is tougher. If my wife submits to me and I choose wrong, she's off the hook with God. She obeyed the Lord by submitting to me. Don't read too much into this. Women should not obey their husbands when doing so would conflict with clear commands in Scripture. But if a wife disagrees with her husband on a gray area of Scripture and submits, then she's *off* the hook and he's *on* the hook.

After explaining how the wife should submit to her husband, Paul explains how the husband should submit to his wife. And what does the husband's submission look like? Love.

"Husbands, love your wives, just as Christ loved the church and gave himself up for her" (Ephesians 5:25).

The kind of love described in this passage isn't some sissy love. This is MAN LOVE! Men, we shouldn't be sissies for Christ. We need to love our wives in the same way that Christ loved us.

Years ago, the television program *All in the Family* reinforced the worst example of love from a husband to his wife. Archie Bunker's wife, Edith, desperately wanted her husband to tell her he loved her. But Archie could only say, "Edith, I've loved you for thirty-eight years. If I change my mind, I'll let you know."

Men all over the country were empowered to keep their mouths shut concerning their love for their wives. That attitude drips with sin!

I hate it when men aren't tough enough to brag on their wives. I hate it even worse when I hear a man insult his wife in front of others. If I hear a preacher insult his wife from the pulpit, everything within me wants to yell, "BOOO!" I can't stand it when men insult their wives. Sometimes I want to slap them... in love, of course!

You see, men are made of iron. Proverbs 27:17 says,

 As iron sharpens iron, so one man sharpens another." Iron is strong, which is why it was used to make swords. If you insult me, it might hurt; but

I'll get over it quickly and ignore you from then on.

Women, on the other hand, are fragile, like porcelain. First Peter 3:7 says,

> Husbands, in the same way be considerate as you live with your wives, and treat them with respect as the *weaker partner* and as heirs with you of the gracious gift of life, so that nothing will hinder your prayers" (italics added).

The phrase "weaker partner" communicates the picture of fine porcelain to me.

If you insult your wife, she will remember it longer than you remember an insult, because you just dropped and shattered her! Porcelain breaks when you drop it. If you drop an iron bowl, you'll just hear a loud CLANK while it bounces on the ground.

We must understand that women are precious pieces of fine china and we cannot insult them—EVER! If you insult your wife, then you are a sissy. We need to MAN UP!

The Extent of Christ's Love for You

God has given us a blueprint for loving our wives. Let's look again at Ephesians 5:25: "Husbands, love your wives, just as Christ loved the church and gave himself up for her."

Men, we need to love our wives in the same way that Christ loved the church. And how did Christ love the church? In chapter 2, I mentioned that I wrote my college senior thesis paper on the medical aspects of the crucifixion. I was given the choice of writing twenty-five pages and defending my paper before the faculty or writing seventy-five pages and just handing it in. I played college football—I didn't have time to write a seventy-five-page paper. But after I started working on it, I couldn't stop, so I ended up writing a seventy-five-page thesis paper, and still defended it!

Several times, while working on my thesis, I ran out of my apartment and into the woods. All alone, I fell on my face and cried out to Jesus, "Why would You allow Yourself to go through such torture?" According to several medical reports in my study, crucifixion was the cruelest torture known to man.

The night before His crucifixion, the soldiers blindfolded Jesus and struck Him in the face several times, mocking Him and telling Him to prophesy who hit Him. Then the next morning the soldiers scourged Him using a whip with several strips of leather at the end. Embedded into the strips were pieces of bone and lead. While the Jews stopped at forty lashes in agreement with Deuteronomy 25:2-3 (thirty-nine lashes, in practice, to be sure they didn't go over the limit), the Romans weren't confined by any limits. When the soldiers were finished, Jesus had lacerations all over his body—on the front as well as the back, from the neck to the top of his knees.

Later the soldiers placed a crown of thorns on His head. The thorns in the "crown" likely came from an acanthus shrub or date palm and were two-and-a-half to three inches long. When placed on His head, the thorns pierced the skin and then recoiled after ramming into His skull, piercing the skin again on the way back out.

Jesus' tormentors forced Him to carry the cross down the street while people mocked and insulted Him. Then they dislocated His shoulders so His arms would stretch across the span of the beam before nailing His hands to the cross. To prevent the nails from tearing through the flesh and freeing Jesus' hands, the soldiers hammered the nails through His wrist, just below the palm. At that spot lies a median nerve that, when severed, sends an excruciating sensation throughout the body. (Did you know that *excruciating* means "out of the cross"?) Jesus felt a similar pain when the nerves in His feet were pierced.

All the while, the crowd mocked and cursed Him. Imagine enduring pain of this magnitude knowing that you have the power to destroy the earth and start completely over. Yet Jesus loved us to the very end of His physical life.

Jesus loves you that much. He willingly died to pay for your sins!

Why did He suffer and die for us? Because He loves us! And He calls us to love our wives in the same way.

Jesus said, "If anyone comes to me and does not hate his father and mother, his wife and children, his brothers and sisters— yes, even his own life—he cannot be my disciple" (Luke 14:26). Our love for anything else in the world should look like hate compared to our love for Jesus.

Since Ephesians 5:25 tells me that I should love my wife as much as Jesus loved me, I figure that my love for anyone or anything (other than God) should look like hatred compared to my love for my wife.

Men, that means you need to love your wives much more than you love golf, hunting, or anything else. Loving your wife is one tangible way to show Jesus that you love Him. And loving your wife becomes much more meaningful to her when you know *how* to love her.

Loving Your Wife

Gary Chapman wrote a significant book called *The Five Love Languages.* In it he describes the different ways every person receives love:

- Touch
- Service
- Encouragement
- Gifts
- Quality time

Look over this list and then place the importance of each love language in order from 1 to 5.

Mine are 1) Touch; 2) Touch; 3) Touch; 4) Encouragement; and 5) Touch. I'm just kidding (a little)! Actually, mine are 1) Touch; 2) Encouragement; 3) Quality time; 4) Gifts; and 5) Service.

Husbands, try to arrange your wife's love languages in order from 1 to 5 without any help from her. Often men are nearly the opposite. After you finish, ask your wife to tell you how you did.

You also need to know that women's love languages tend to change over time (though men's usually do not). That means we continually need to adjust to our wives' ever-changing love languages.

Have you ever heard of the one-year, seven-year, and twenty-one-year itch? Marriages more often end in divorce during those years. Perhaps those "itches" appear after our wives' love languages have changed. Since ours rarely change, we expect them to be like us; so we keep dong the same thing without realizing that we're no longer loving our wives very well.

In a sense, we need to stalk our wives, like a hunter stalks a deer. We need to hunt for our wives' love languages.

All too often we love our wives according to *our* list of love languages. Touch is usually number 1 for most men and number 5 for most women. If we primarily show love to our wives through touch, then we aren't really loving our wives very well, if at all—certainly not like Christ.

You need to love your wife according to *her* list of love languages. Let's say that service is number 5 on your list and number 1 on her list. If you want to love her like Christ loved the church, then you need to train yourself to make the bed for her—if she loves having the bed made for her—even if you hate doing it. Eventually you'll get to the point where you love making the bed, and it becomes *your* love language.

Love Means to Give ... and Give Again

People say that marriage is all about give and take. That's garbage. Love is give... and give... and give again.

On the night Jesus was betrayed, unimaginable acts were committed against Him. He was beaten, abused, and mocked. And then the next day He was forced to carry His own cross to Golgotha. Then He was stripped naked and nailed to a tree. Yet after all this, Jesus prayed, "Father, forgive them, for they do not know what they are doing" (Luke 23:34).

That's give-and-give love. It's selfless. The real thing.

I know of a man whose wife left him at home to take care of their four kids while she spent many nights drinking in bars and messing around with other guys. Several years later, she came home one night and fell down on her face and cried, "Why do you still love me?"

"Because I love Jesus," he said, "and I'm being obedient to Him."

That night she gave her life to Christ, and she is still serving Him!

Husbands, loving your wife means being wronged and admitting you're wrong. Through trial and error, I've learned the twelve key words to bringing an end to every argument: "I am sorry. Please forgive me. I love you. I was wrrrrrrrrrrrrrrrrrrrrrrrrrrong."

Now you may be saying, "Hey! What if I didn't do anything wrong?" Even if the wife is 100 percent wrong, the husband is still wrong because he is at least partly responsible for his wife losing her cool and getting into an argument. He needs to be the head of the household and lead by saying he's sorry. Many new husbands have trouble with this one until about their fifth argument.

Phew—that's tough to say! I have used those twelve words often and they work every time!! Practice them right now so you can say them before, during, and after your next argument.

Treat Her Like an Eight-Cow Wife

As Paul continues calling husbands to love their wives the way Christ loved the church, he writes that Christ gave Himself up for her in order to "present her to himself as a radiant church, without stain or wrinkle or any other blemish, but holy and blameless" (Ephesians 5:27).

Jesus' goal is to make us radiant, without stain, wrinkle, or any blemish. What a great example for us men to follow with our wives!

I once heard a story about a shrewd businessman who lived on an island in the Pacific. On this island chain men paid for their wives, and the currency they used was cows. The businessman traveled to a neighboring island to approach a man about marrying his daughter.

The young woman was homely and suffered from extremely low self-esteem. Her father knew he would only get one cow out of the shrewd businessman, but he still asked for two. Yet, to his amazement the businessman offered eight cows. Everyone on the island knew the father had taken advantage of the businessman, which destroyed his reputation for being shrewd.

A year later a friend of the father visited the young woman on the neighboring island and couldn't believe his eyes. She was breathtaking. Shoulders back, walking tall, beautifully styled hair—all in all, she was gorgeous!

"What happened to your wife?" the family friend asked.

"If you want an eight-cow wife," the man replied with a smile, "then you should pay eight cows for her."

If you want an eight-cow wife, then treat her with great respect and honor and she'll become one. Brag about her like she is a trophy!

Finally, Paul concludes his comments about marriage by explaining, "Husbands ought to love their wives as their own bodies. He who loves his wife loves himself" (Ephesians 5:28).

Here's the mystery of marriage. When you think only of yourself—when you place work or pleasure ahead of your wife —your life is miserable. Your wife nags you to spend more time with her. You fight a lot, and you never seem to have enough time to do what you want to do. No one is happy.

But when you truly love your wife, you enjoy being with each other and you don't fight nearly as much, and she enjoys giving you time to hunt or do whatever else because she knows you really care about her.

You see, Paul was right. When you love your wife, you love yourself.

Men, we need to learn out how to love our wives—not only for our wives and ourselves, but also for our kids who need it modeled in their lives.

 **TOOL BOX**

1. *Love takes the sting out of sacrifice.* Does this convict you? It should.

2. As soon as possible, ask your wife to tell you what her love languages are.

3. Ask your wife to give you a list of what you need to do to love her according to her love languages.

4. Practice the twelve key words to marriage after an argument: "I am sorry. Please forgive me. I love you. I was wrrrrrrrrrrrrrrrrrrrong." One time I had trouble saying the last line to my wife. Finally, she gestured at me, kind of like the way people do when they call a dog to come into the house. As she waved me to come home, I mumbled the last three words!! UGH! Once they came out, I felt instant relief!!!

CHRISTIAN MAN LAW #12

REAL CHRISTIAN MEN PLAY THEIR POSITION

My senior year in college we played a football game against a team we needed to beat in order to win the conference title. I played defensive end, lining up across from the opposing team's all-conference tight end.

Their favorite play was the "toss sweep," in which the tight end's job was to block me. I could tell when they were about to run the play because the tight end would move his hand back in his stance. As a result, we stopped them cold every time they ran that play. I also sacked the quarterback a couple of times, along with making several tackles. It was the game of my life.

Toward the end of the game we were winning by two points, and the other team was unable to move the ball against us. The coach called a blitz, which meant I was supposed to rush the quarterback on an inside maneuver. However, the tight end moved his hand back in his stance, so I thought they were going to run the "toss sweep." If I blitzed and the other team ran a "toss sweep," they'd be able to run around me and make a sizable gain.

I'll never forget what I did next. Disobeying the coach's instructions, I didn't blitz inside; instead, I ran straight outside so I could stop prevent the sweep. The running back shot through the gigantic hole where I should have been and ran for sixty-nine yards. The next play they kicked a field goal and beat us. Because I didn't play my position, we lost the game.

Real Christian men play their position.

Play Your Position

Every player on defense has a gap responsibility. If one person wants to be a star by taking a different gap, the defense breaks down. If two people cover one gap, then another gap won't be covered. Usually a big play on offense comes from a gap that wasn't occupied on defense.

I volunteer as a defensive line coach on my son's high school football team. Getting players who refuse to listen or who insist on doing their own thing to play as a team is difficult. Extremely difficult.

Imagine how God feels trying to get all of us to play our position.

> Now the body is not made up of one part but of many. If the foot should say, "Because I am not a hand, I do not belong to the body," it would not for that reason cease to be a part of the body.
>
> 1 CORINTHIANS 12:14-15

Everybody is given a different but equally important position. If you're unhappy with the position you're playing, that doesn't mean you're not on the team.

If the whole body were an eye, where would the sense of hearing be? If the whole body were an ear, where would the sense of smell be? But in fact *God has arranged the parts of the body, every one of them, just as he wanted them to be.*

1 CORINTHIANS 12:17-18 (ITALICS ADDED)

If everyone played wide receiver, who would pass the ball? An offensive lineman is just as important to a pass play as the wide receiver. We need to trust that the coach has placed every player in the position that suits him best.

The eye cannot say to the hand, "I don't need you!" And the head cannot say to the feet, "I don't need you!"

1 CORINTHIANS 12:21

Contrary to the way our culture operates, the parts that seem to be weaker are actually indispensable (1 Corinthians 12:22). The "weaker" gifts, though, operate behind the scenes. Most people esteem the mouth, the part that's up-front and visible. Or they look up to the gift of leadership. Everyone values the up-front gifts over the backstage gifts.

However, the weaker gifts are considered indispensable. Without them, the body of Christ can barely function. We cannot work as a team without every link in the chain. Scripture doesn't say that the gift of evangelist is indispensable, but it does say that the weaker gifts are. I love the way that God considers the hidden gifts like service, encouragement, and hospitality to be necessary.

Imagine the star quarterback telling his offensive line, "I don't need you." After getting pummeled for two or three plays because his blockers decided to take a breather, you better believe he'd come crawling on his knees begging for their help.

If you aren't happy with your gifts, trust that God knows what He is doing. Every gift that He gives fits perfectly in the body of Christ.

God Has Designed You with Unique Gifts

God deliberately gave you a unique mix of gifts. You had no choice in the matter, but in His infinite wisdom He knew what gifts would work best with your personality and His calling on your life.

Imagine what would happen if the nose guard and free safety switched positions. You see, nose guards rarely get noticed, but free safeties make the big plays. Nose guards are huge, and their job is to force teams to double-team them. When they can draw a double-team, another defensive lineman will line up against a single blocker. Because defensive linemen are usually quicker than offensive linemen, they can run past a single player and make the tackle. But if the leaner, lighter free safety starts playing nose guard, he won't draw the second offensive linesman, giving the offense a better chance of making a big play. Imagine a nose guard playing the free safety position. He'll lack the speed to cover a fleet-footed receiver coming out of the backfield.

Sportswriters never praise the nose guard who drew double-teams all night. You just read about the defensive ends on either side who made all the tackles and the free safety who made the big plays (hopefully!).

This happens all too often in the body of Christ. People with the gift of encouragement or the gift of service are similar to the nose guard on the defensive line. Few people notice them because the fivefold offices in the church (apostles, prophets, evangelists, pastors, and teachers), mentioned in Ephesians 4:11, get most of the attention. But without men and women who encourage and serve, the body of Christ wouldn't function properly.

I don't have an organizational bone in my body. Five times I've missed a speaking event because I forgot about it. You know why? I booked them myself instead of booking them through Kingdom Building Ministries (KBM), the ministry I work with. Loren Hayes works with KBM, and his full-time job is to organize the schedules of each of their speakers. He's worth his weight in gold, but no one sees him on stage.

Loren once told me that God called him to administrate me as a preacher. I believe him! I speak about two hundred days a year, and he organizes my life. What would I do without him?

In their infinite wisdom, Forge: Kingdom Building Ministries hired my wife, Lisa, to organize the ministry in my home, so she can get me out the door and headed in the right direction. Lisa works ten hours a week on that job. Her gift is administration as well.

One time on a flight, our family was bumped up to first class. One parent, though, would have to sit apart from the rest of the family while the other cared for the kids. I said to Lisa, "Why don't you take a break from the kids and sit in row 4 next to that person?"

Do you know how she responded to my generous offer? "I'd rather be tied to a herd of buffaloes and dragged across the prairie than sit next to a stranger!"

I love sitting next to strangers and talking to them about Jesus, but it would kill Lisa. God has given everyone a unique set of gifts.

What Energizes You?

You can usually tell what your gifts are by asking yourself what you love to do. If you love encouraging people, then your gift is encouragement. If you love organizing things, then your gift is administration, etc.

When I say you "love" using your spiritual gift, I mean that you feel energized when you exercise it. I realize that personality types affect this to varying degrees, but the energy you feel goes beyond personality types. If you have the gift of hospitality, then you get energized about the opportunity to host people in your home.

As someone whom God has gifted as an evangelist, people approach me all the time saying they want to be an evangelist too. I think people look at evangelists on a stage and want to imitate them on the stage as well. Perhaps an evangelist played a significant role in their lives in the past and they see it as an opportunity to help people in the same way. That doesn't mean they have the gift of evangelism, though.

The same applies to any spiritual gift.

Although I can't prove it in Scripture, I believe God gives every person the propensity for their specific gifts at birth. After we give our lives to Christ, these gifts come to the forefront. While we should be thankful for the gifts He's given us, we can also pray that God would give us the "greater gifts" (1 Corinthians 12:31), which Paul explains in 1 Corinthians 14.

Your Position on the Team Is Important

Why are spiritual gifts so important to the body of Christ?

Jesus said, in Matthew 9:37-38, "The harvest is plentiful, but the laborers are few; therefore pray earnestly to the Lord of the harvest to send out laborers into his harvest" (ESV).

We need to ask God to send more laborers into the harvest field because the harvest is ready to be brought in and the laborers are few. My definition of a laborer is someone who uses his gifts. We don't need to envy other people's gifts. Otherwise, how would we work together as a team?

This is one of the most important passages in the Bible. Although our gifts differ, all Christians are called to be laborers. The harvest is at stake. God has positioned every person, however, in the right spot. He has set up a perfect system for reaping the harvest. Every Christian has been given at least one spiritual gift—and when we use our gifts, the harvest *will* be brought in.

What an amazing system!!!

Although my football team lost an important game, in part because I didn't play my position, we still made the playoffs. Later, in the semifinals, we played another close game, and I lined up against a giant tight end. He was so big his number was 179. Just kidding!

It was fourth down and the other team had the ball six inches from our goal line. If we stopped them, we would probably win. If we didn't, the game and our season might be over.

Our defensive captain gave us the play, which told us where we should line up. This time I decided to play my position. When the ball was snapped, the offensive tackle and tight end lunged at both the defensive tackle and me. But because we played our positions, we knew what to do. When the play was over, we had stuffed the linemen in front of us and tackled the running back who was carrying the ball. We won the game!

When everyone plays their position, the body of Christ plays as a team and we win.

Men, let's play our positions!

 **TOOL BOX**

Here are some ideas to help you determine your spiritual gifts:

1. Do whatever you can to draw closer to Christ. His will for your life will become evident as you delight yourself in Him. That's why Psalm 37:4 tells us, "Delight yourself in the Lord and he will give you the desires of your heart." If you delight yourself in the Lord and earnestly desire to know your gifts, He'll show them to you. Why wouldn't that be His desire too?

2. Go online and type "spiritual gifts evaluation" into a search engine. You'll be able to find a number of inventories that can help you get a good idea of what your gifts are. Take an evaluation as soon as you can so that you can start investing while the market is right!!

3. Spend time sifting through the following passages to learn more about what God's Word says about spiritual gifts:

- Romans 12:1-8
- 1 Corinthians 12–14
- Ephesians 4:7-16
- 1 Peter 4:10-11

4. Ask people in your Christian community what they think your spiritual gifts are—then compare that with the results of your gifts evaluation and your own personal study.

CHRISTIAN MAN LAW #13

CHRISTIAN MEN WORK FOR A SABBATH REST

YOU'RE DRIVING UP A MOUNTAIN ROAD AND AS YOU COME OVER the crest you see a highway patrol officer pointing his radar gun at you. You look down at your speedometer and see that you're driving ten miles over the speed limit.

What is running through your head?

For the next seventeen miles, are you watching your rearview mirrors rather than the road, knowing that at any point he could be on you like white on rice? Is your heart breaking the speed limit? Is your blood pressure racing through the roof? One thing's for sure: you have no peace. Am I right?

On the contrary, how would you feel if you crested the same mountain, saw the same highway patrol officer pointing his radar gun at you, looked down at your speedometer, and saw that you were driving the speed limit? Would you still jerk your foot off the gas? (Probably—me too!) However, after realizing that you were going the speed limit, imagine how much you would enjoy the next seventeen miles. Perfect peace! Am I right?

That is the perfect picture of Sabbath rest. Actually, the Sabbath has nothing to do with taking a nap on a Sunday afternoon, or even directly with Sunday alone. Even though the Old Testament Sabbath occurred on Saturday, eventually the New Testament church changed their Sabbath to Sunday because Jesus rose from the dead on the first day of the week.

God's idea of Sabbath rest, however, applies to every day of the week. It applies to all of us, men!

The Greek word *sabbatismos*, translated "Sabbath rest" or "Sabbath-rest," is only found in one place in the New Testament. Hebrews 4:9-11 says,

> For if Joshua had given [the Israelites] rest, God would not have spoken later about another day. There remains, then, a *Sabbath-rest* for the people of God; for anyone who enters God's rest also rests from his own work, just as God did from his. Let us, therefore, make every effort to enter that rest, so that no one will fall by following their example of disobedience (italics added).

Earlier, the writer of Hebrews explained that God, after creating the world, rested on the seventh day (Hebrews 4:4). God has been resting since then, and He wants us to join Him.

Doesn't the Sabbath-rest life sound good to you? Perfect peace in the middle of any storm. The feeling of relief that comes from knowing you aren't going to get a speeding ticket. If so, then you need to understand the context of this passage and apply it.

Jesus Is Better

The Romans, fed up with the Jews in Jerusalem, took measures to quell their rebellion in AD 70. It is my understanding that as the Jews prepared for the Roman general Titus (who would soon became emperor) to arrive and lay siege to the city, Jewish Christians began contemplating a return to the Jewish faith. After all, God would not allow His city to fall, would He? The letter to the Hebrews was written to caution against that decision to revert to Judaism.

The theme of the book is that Jesus is superior to the old covenant, the Jewish system of beliefs that we read about in the Old Testament (see Hebrews 7:22):

- Jesus is superior to the angels (chapter 1)
- Jesus is superior to the Jews' esteemed leader, Moses (chapter 3)
- Jesus is superior to the high priest (chapters 4-5)
- Jesus' priesthood is superior to the Jewish priesthood (chapter 7)
- Jesus is a better sacrifice than any animal sacrifice (chapters 9-10)

Through Moses, God instituted what Jews called "the law," a code of beliefs and practices that required repeated animal sacrifices. Jesus, however, by sacrificing Himself on the cross, offered complete forgiveness without the requirement of any more animals (Hebrews 7:27; 10:4).

Let's take another look at Hebrews 4:11:

> Let us, therefore, make every effort to enter that rest, so that no one will fall by following their example of disobedience.

The author mentions rest as the opposite of disobedience.

Disobedience to what, though? It's a reference to the events in Numbers 13 and 14. This is a good example of what Sabbath rest is, and isn't.

Beware of the Deadly Little Word

God told the Israelites to spy out the promised land of Canaan, so Moses sent twelve spies, including Joshua and Caleb. When they entered the land, they couldn't believe their eyes. The clusters of grapes were so huge that two men were needed to carry them.

Earlier God had described the land to Moses as "flowing with milk and honey" (Exodus 3:8). That means the cows and goats were fat and well-fed, so they produced plenty of milk. Honey was plentiful because bees were plentiful, which meant that they were busy pollinating the crops. That, in turn, meant the land was fertile and the crops were abundant. We're talking plenty of meat and potatoes.

After forty days the spies returned and reported back to Moses, "We went into the land to which you sent us, and it does flow with milk and honey!" (Numbers 13:27). They seemed surprised that God was right. The land was truly flowing with milk and honey.

Then they said something that robbed all of Israel from the Sabbath rest of God. Actually, it's the one word that undermines God's promise of a Sabbath rest to all of us.

Quite often you can underline that word in your Bible because you know something bad is about to happen. It's a short word, rich in negativity. Here it is...

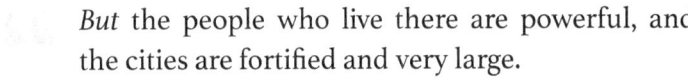

> *But* the people who live there are powerful, and
> the cities are fortified and very large.

NUMBERS 13:28, ITALICS ADDED

The men began by telling the truth: the promised land was fertile and rich, just as God said. Then they added that deadly little word: *but*.

They began listing the different tribes of people they would need to fight: the Hittites, the Jebusites, the Amalekites, the Goflyakites (I made that one up). Even the descendants of Anak, who were giants compared to them.

You get the point. They were reluctant. Worse, they were terrified.

We Need to Know, Believe, and Do

God had promised that He would drive out the Israelites' enemies. He was their God and they were His people. They belonged to Him.

When God says something about you, how many times out of 100 is He right? If your answer is 100, you're wrong. You should give Him 5 bonus points, just in case you think He might be wrong, because He's always right. Always. So you should give Him a 105.

On the other hand, how many times out of 100 are you right when you disagree with God? Minus 5 is the right answer—because even when you think you're right and God is wrong, God is still right. Again, He deserves 5 bonus points.

Do you know how I define low self-esteem? Believing the minus 5! Disagreeing with what God says about you, which is the opposite of Sabbath rest.

Thankfully, two spies believed what God said about them. We read in Numbers 13:30: "Then Caleb silenced the people before Moses and said, 'We should go up and take possession of the land, for we can certainly do it.'"

Caleb knew that the people, through God, could overcome their enemies. He knew it wasn't the *promise* land, it was the *promised* land. Past tense. God had *already* given it to them. Canaan already belonged to the Israelites.

That's what Sabbath rest is: confidence in God's Word and feeling peace as you obey Him.

Sabbath rest is knowing the Word, believing the Word, and doing the Word.

But there was one problem. No one was listening to Caleb and his friend Joshua. The other ten men allowed that little word *but*—instead of God's promise—to rule them. Those men, obviously, didn't live in Sabbath rest.

Word of the majority opinion spread like the plague, instilling fear in everyone. Giants were everywhere, the ten exclaimed. "We saw the Nephilim there (the descendants of Anak come from the Nephilim). We seemed like grasshoppers in our own eyes, and we looked the same to them" (Numbers 13:33).

How pathetic is that? You know what bugs me the most about their words? It's not like they walked up to the gigantic Nephilim and said, "Hey, excuse me, what do I look like to you —a grasshopper?" No, that conversation never happened. They said, "We seemed like grasshoppers *in our own eyes*," revealing that they were being deceived by self-esteem issues.

The spies' belief about themselves resembled that of a well-known leader later in Israel's history. He too had a hard time believing what God said about him.

You're a Mighty Warrior—Not the Biggest Loser

Gideon was threshing wheat in a winepress, trying to prevent the Midianites, Israel's oppressors, from stealing it. The walls of the winepress hid what he was doing, but they made threshing wheat difficult, because you need wind to blow the chaff away from the grain.

The angel of the Lord appeared to Gideon and said, "The Lord is with you, mighty warrior" (Judges 6:12). Mighty warrior? Gideon was acting like a chicken. But notice that the angel also reminded Gideon that God was with him. Most Bible scholars believe the angel was the preincarnate Christ—i.e., the Son of God before He was born to Mary.

If you think you're a chicken, when God says you're a mighty warrior and that He's on your side, who are you going to believe —you or God?

We all do the same thing. We second-guess ourselves in an assortment of creative ways when God has affirmed us. If you've been born again by the Spirit of God, it doesn't matter what you think about yourself. God says you're a mighty warrior right now. Right. Now. You are a stud in Christ.

Here's how deep-seated Gideon's low self-esteem was. The angel of the Lord appeared to him and told him God was with him, yet Gideon responded by saying—watch this: "'*But* sir,' Gideon replied, 'if the Lord is with us, why has all this happened to us?'" (Judges 6:13, italics added). There's that deadly little word again.

Gideon continued by explaining he came from the weakest family in the weakest clan of his tribe. Gideon claimed to be the original *biggest loser.*

Then God put an end to Gideon's pathetic excuses: "I will be with you, and you will strike down all the Midianites together" (verse 16).

Gideon still refused to believe God. Instead, he challenged Him to a test and asked for a sign. Gideon is talking to God Almighty and he's asking for more proof!! Gideon prepared a sacrifice, and then the angel of the Lord touched it with his staff and the whole thing went up in smoke. Gideon, realizing now that he had been talking to the angel of the Lord, cried out that he was going to die.

The angel told Gideon to peel himself off of the ground, because he wasn't going to die. Gideon was weak-minded. He didn't understand the power of having God on his side.

But that's not all; there's more. Later Gideon insisted on testing God again. One night he laid a wool fleece on the threshing floor and asked God to make the fleece wet and the ground around it dry the next morning. God answered his request. (This was probably fun for God. Maybe.)

Yet Gideon *still* wasn't convinced. So, just to be sure, the next night he laid the wool fleece on the threshing floor and asked God to keep the fleece dry and make the ground around it wet. God *again* answered his request.

Finally, Gideon decided to obey.

Has someone ever told you that we should lay our fleece before the Lord to determine His will? Really, that's the heart of a chicken. Don't be like Gideon. You'll never experience God's Sabbath rest when you keep asking for more proof. If God tells you to do something, then do it.

Convinced, Gideon mobilized the army to fight. He began with 32,000 men, but God said he had too many. He pared the army down to 10,000, but God said the army was still too big. Mind you, Gideon's men were fighting an army of 135,000 Midianites. Eventually God whittled the troops down to 300 men. I'm not very good at math, but 300 against 135,000 doesn't seem very fair.

In the end, Gideon and his army stood in the hills surrounding the Midianites, blowing their trumpets and yelling, which threw the enemy into confusion. They either destroyed each other with their swords or fled from the camp, making themselves an easy target for the Israelites. God gave Gideon and His people a great victory.

How often do we resemble Gideon by failing to believe what God says about us, about our circumstances, and about what He will do?

Entering God's Sabbath Rest Gives You More Than Happiness

Now let's return to our story about the ten men's report after spying out the promised land. After listening to the ten men, the people began clamoring to turn around and go back to Egypt. They wanted to give up the idea of entering the promised land, pick a new leader, and return to their lives of slavery.

That is what the author of Hebrews is talking about. That's the "example of disobedience."

 Let us, therefore, make every effort to enter that rest, so that no one will fall by following their example of disobedience.

HEBREWS 4:11

Joshua and Caleb pleaded with the people, "If the Lord is pleased with us, he will lead us into that land, a land flowing with milk and honey, and will give it to us" (Numbers 14:8).

Compare Gideon with Joshua and Caleb. Gideon needed multiple confirmations before deciding to lead Israel against the Midianites. Joshua and Caleb saw giants in the land but believed God's assessment of them is right 105 times out of 100.

Joshua, Caleb, Moses, Aaron, and the writer of Hebrews knew that when you're in the center of God's will you experience joy (which is different than happiness) that makes work EASY.

When you *know* God's Word intimately, *believe* God's Word wholeheartedly, and *obey* God's Word immediately, you enter His Sabbath rest. You sense an energy and excitement inside you.

Men, let's study it, believe it, and do it!

Have you ever decided to disobey God? Of course you have. Doesn't your decision make you feel horrible?

Have you ever decided to obey God? I hope you have. Doesn't your decision make you feel good?

One night at 2 a.m. on the way home from an event, I stopped at a convenience store. I told the guy behind the counter that Jesus was thinking about him at that moment.

"How do you know that?" he asked.

"Because the Bible says He is," I replied. "And He's fond of you; He thinks you're awesome."

I shared the gospel with him, and he gave his life to Christ. Right after we finished praying together, three cars drove up. I said, "God kept those three cars from coming, or I wouldn't have shared with you."

"Man, my grandmother's going to be glad to hear about what happened tonight." That was beautiful music to my ears, because, like I said earlier in this book, I want to be the answer to some grandmother's prayer.

I walked out of that store on a high—it was better than any drug I ever abused earlier in my life. The energy and excitement that comes from knowing, believing, and doing God's Word is the closest you'll ever get to flying without an airplane.

I wrote this song...

> *Trust and obey,*
> *For there's no other way,*
> *To be happy,*
> *victorious, overwhelmed with joy, walking smack-dab in the*
> *middle of God's will,*
> *in Jesus,*
> *Than to trust and obey.*

Actually, I only wrote the fourth line. The original song, "Trust and Obey," is a little cheesy. The song promises that when we trust and obey God we'll be "happy in Jesus." I want to be more than just happy. When you trust and obey, you get peace. Real peace. Sabbath rest peace. But you'll also be victorious and overwhelmed with joy.

All this comes from knowing you're walking smack-dab in the center of God's will. You're knowing God's Word, believing God's Word, and doing God's Word.

After urging us to make every effort to enter God's rest through obedience, the writer of Hebrews tells us:

> The word of God is living and active. Sharper than any double-edged sword, it penetrates even to dividing soul and spirit, joints and marrow; it judges the thoughts and attitudes of the heart.
>
> HEBREWS 4:12

The Word of God is living and active. Studying it leads to believing it and then doing it.

Hebrews 5:14 says that "solid food is for the mature, who because of *practice*"—constant use—"have their senses *trained* to discern good and evil" (NASB, italics added).

That's the key to Sabbath rest. You know the Word and you do it. You practice the Word and God leads you into His promised land of Sabbath rest.

Men, let's get after it!

TOOL BOX

1. Remember that Sabbath rest applies to every day of the week. It doesn't mean you stop working. It simply means that while you are working you have peace.

2. Think about a time in your life when you made an unwise decision. What Scripture passage comes to mind that would have helped you make a better choice?

3. Read a passage from the New Testament TODAY, and then do what it says.

4. Go out and enjoy a big, fat, juicy steak in the Word!

CHRISTIAN MAN LAW #14

CHRISTIAN MEN LEAVE A LEGACY

"The merchant of death is dead!" read the obituary in the French newspaper in 1888. Ludvig Nobel had died, but the newspaper mistakenly published the obituary of his well-known brother Alfred. The obituary described Nobel as a man "who became rich by finding ways to kill more people faster than ever before."

When Alfred Nobel learned that he would be remembered as the "merchant of death," he was devastated. You see, the man was famous for inventing dynamite. He owned ammunition factories around the world and was a major contributor to every war.

After this ordeal, he decided to change his legacy. Seven years later, just before his death, he set aside the equivalent of $250 million to fund an annual prize that would be awarded to outstanding individuals in five categories, the most famous being the Nobel Peace Prize.

More than one hundred years later, Alfred Nobel is known as a man of peace, not of war.

The Problem with Our Past

We tend to beat ourselves up about our past. Yet no matter how hard we try, we cannot change it. We *can* change our future, however. We can change the legacy we're leaving behind.

Steve Caswell, a dear friend of mine, passed away from nonsmoker's lung cancer. His death reminded me of the frailty of life and of my own eventual death.

Have you ever thought about your death? It might seem morbid, but it's part of the deal that comes with life. Someday you *will* die. What will your legacy be?

Steve left behind a legacy of generosity and service. At his funeral, the large church sanctuary was brimming with people Steve had touched. Person after person remarked after the service that whenever someone asked Steve for help, he gave his trademark reply: "Absolutely, without a doubt!" What a legacy.

Most of us base our decisions on the finite instead of the infinite. We live in the here and now when we could be living with eternity in mind. All of us will leave behind a legacy, but the best legacies begin with heaven rather than earth.

Five Ways to Ensure a Godly Legacy

If you want to leave behind a life-satisfying, God-glorifying legacy, then consider these five steps.

1. *Make sure you're born again*

One of my concerns is that a great number of people believe they are saved when they have no apparent evidence to back up their claim. This is the spiritual equivalent of the bubonic plague in our country. I believe millions of Americans fall into this category.

I think this problem exists because our definition of the word *believe* has changed since Jesus' day. This isn't unusual, since the meanings of words change over time. After hearing me speak, teenagers will tell me, "Thanks for getting all up in my grill!" When I was their age, getting up in someone's grill meant jumping on top of their barbecue! Or after a meeting someone might tell me that my message was "sick," which is actually a compliment. Meanings change.

But it's extremely dangerous to begin changing the meaning of Jesus' words, and it affects whether or not we'll make it to heaven.

Are you sure you believe? What do you think Jesus meant when He said "believe"? In my personal study, I have only found one place in Scripture where the word *believe* is defined. If you believe according to this definition, then you are going to heaven. If not, then you won't go to heaven.

In John 3, Jesus declared to a Pharisee named Nicodemus that "no one can see the kingdom of God unless he is born again" (verse 3).

What does it mean to be born again?

Being Born Again Is Intense!

If you have children, were you in the delivery room when your kids were born? I was with my wife during the birth of all four of our kids. Lisa is as tough as nails. I mean, she's tough. When she bowls, she throws overhand!!

When she gave birth to our first child, she said she wanted to go "natural." I didn't know what that meant. I thought she was talking about a baseball movie. (Pretty good show!) Later I learned it meant that she didn't want to use any drugs to dull the pain.

The nurses attached her to this seismograph thing that measured her earthquakes. No, not real earthquakes—the earthquakes in her body. It measured the strength of her contractions.

The higher the needle pointed, the louder she screamed. On one contraction the needle went straight to the top.

"Lisa," I said, "that's a big one!"

She screamed at me—and I quote: "SHUUUUUUUUUUT UUUUUUUUPPPPPPPP!!" She squeezed my hand so hard that my knuckle popped out. So I yelled! Then the midwife, who weighed about a buck twenty-five, screamed at me to shut up.

I have experienced some very intense situations in my life, but nothing compares to watching my wife give birth without drugs to ease her pain.

Very intense! And that's how intense being born again should be.

Jesus said that we must be born again for good reason: it's tough and intense!

Nicodemus then asked Jesus, "How can I be born at my age? It's not like I can jump back into my mother's womb and exit a second time!"

Jesus then dropped on him what I call the Gospel Bomb. To my knowledge, this is the only place in the Bible where the word *believe* is defined. Jesus answered,

> Just as Moses lifted up the snake in the desert, so the Son of Man must be lifted up, that everyone who believes in him may have eternal life.

JOHN 3:14-15

Jesus' analogy might seem confusing to you, but Nicodemus knew exactly what He meant. As a religious leader in Israel, he had likely told this story several times.

The Israelites had wandered in the desert for 38 years of their 40-year prison sentence. Once again, they began grumbling about eating manna every day. At this point, nearly everyone who had lived in Egypt was dead. All this younger generation knew was manna. Nevertheless, they began complaining about "this miserable food" and "spoke against God and against Moses, and said, 'Why have you brought us up out of Egypt to die in the desert?'" (Numbers 21:5).

So God sent venomous snakes into their camp, likely sand vipers, which are common in the area. The snakes bit the people and many of them died a violent, painful death.

Imagine watching helplessly as some of your best friends die from a snake bite. The Israelites finally came to their senses and cried out to Moses, "We sinned when we spoke against the Lord and against you. Pray that the Lord will take the snakes away from us" (Numbers 21:7).

Moses prayed, and God instructed him to construct a snake out of bronze and put it up on a pole. Everyone bitten by a snake who looked at the sculpture would be healed.

Keep Your Eyes on the Snake on the Pole

Why didn't God simply remove the snakes? He wanted to give the people a tangible illustration of the word *believe*.

Imagine that you've been bitten by a snake. If you were about to die and your back was turned to the statue, how quickly would you turn around and face it if you believed it would heal you? Immediately. If you were miles away, would you walk through the hot desert to be saved? Absolutely!

Jesus is comparing the word *believe* to the passion of a dying man who will do anything to get healed.

Years ago I took my youth group to a water park and spent some time swimming in the wave pool with one of the kids. The boy wanted to see who could swim in the middle of the pool the longest without using a floaty. He didn't tell me he wasn't a very good swimmer!

Once the waves started throwing us around, the boy grabbed onto my neck for dear life and we both sank to the bottom. Somehow I bubbled out the words, "What are you doing?"

I untangled his arms from my neck and held him over my head so he could breathe in between the waves. Then I leaned forward and started walking on the floor toward the side of the giant wave pool, hoisting him above the water. The lifeguards saw us and pulled him out, but they forgot about me.

At the bottom of the pool, I bubbled again, "What about meeeee?" I knew that if I didn't act soon, I would drown; so I kicked myself out of the water one last time as hard as I could and lunged for the side rail. As a wave lifted me up to the rail, I grabbed it before the wave passed by. Then I held on for dear life. I knew that if I let go I would probably drown, so I focused all of my attention on clinging to the railing.

That, my dear friends, is the scriptural definition of the word *believe*. It means believing as if your life depends on it, which it does. You believe so strongly that no NFL defensive lineman could pry you away from the railing.

You Can Be Saved

With this in mind, let's look again at Jesus' words in John 3:14-15:

> Just as Moses lifted up the snake in the desert, so the Son of Man must be lifted up, that everyone who believes in him may have eternal life.

Jesus compared Himself to the bronze snake on the pole *when He is lifted up*. In the Gospel of John, the phrase "lifted up" means to be crucified. In John 12:32, Jesus said, "But I, when I am lifted up from the earth, will draw all men to myself." John then explained that Jesus said this to show the kind of death He was going to die.

There it is! Just like the Israelites believed by looking at the snake on the pole, so we must believe by looking to Jesus and depending entirely on Him to save us from certain death. That's what it means to be born again! Believing in Jesus involves more than just mastering a set of facts about a man who lived two thousand years ago. It means everything within you wants Him!

All of us have been bitten by a snake called sin. Without help, we will all die. But when we turn to Jesus and look to Him to save us, we'll be saved.

Have you been saved? Have you been born again? Has your life been changed?

If you haven't been born again, you can turn to Jesus right now. Just pray this prayer and *believe*:

> Lord Jesus, I know that I have sinned against You many times, and I am very sorry. I have lied, stolen, lusted, (confess whatever sins come to your mind), etc. Please forgive me. I want to truly believe in You now. I give You all that I am. Thank You for dying for me. I want to live for You! In Jesus' name, Amen.

If you just prayed that prayer, then welcome home!

That's the first step in leaving a legacy. After that...

2. Develop a passion for souls

In the Scriptures, words or phrases were repeated for emphasis. If it was repeated twice, it was important. Three times, and it was absolutely true. That's why the angelic creatures surrounding the throne of God cried, "Holy, holy, holy" (Isaiah 6:3; Revelation 4:8).

Paul introduces an important statement with these words in Romans 9:1:

 I speak the truth in Christ—I am not lying, my conscience confirms it in the Holy Spirit.

By essentially repeating himself three times, Paul is trying to tell his readers that what he is about to say is extremely important...

"I have great sorrow and unceasing anguish in my heart" (Romans 9:2).

What he is about to say is crushing his soul. For a brief moment, he is about to give his readers a window into his heart...

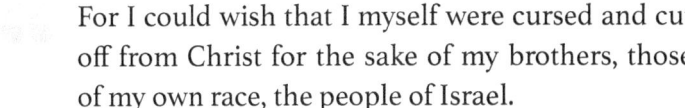

> For I could wish that I myself were cursed and cut off from Christ for the sake of my brothers, those of my own race, the people of Israel.
>
> ROMANS 9:3-4

What? Paul would go to hell for the Jews? They had beaten him several times (see 2 Corinthians 11:24). Would you be willing to go to hell for someone who had beaten and rejected you? I have wrestled with this passage for several years, and it continues to challenge me. Do I want people to get saved so badly that I would be willing to go to hell for them? I'm not sure.

Paul knew what heaven was like and had seen and heard inexpressible things that he was not allowed to discuss (2 Corinthians 12:1-6). To prevent him from becoming conceited after getting a foretaste of heaven, a demon was sent to torment him (2 Corinthians 12:7). Paul describes his thorn in the flesh as a "messenger of Satan." The word for "messenger" is literally translated "angel." An angel of Satan is a demon. Wow! Paul's experience with heaven was so intense that he needed a demon to prevent him from getting a big head.

Yet Paul said that he would exchange heaven for the salvation of the people who beat him and made his life physically miserable.

Imagine what kind of legacy you would leave if you shared Paul's passion for souls.

3. Refuse the demonic double take

Do you know what the word *devil* literally means? Accuser. In fact, Scripture describes the devil as "the accuser of our brothers, who accuses them before our God day and night" (Revelation 12:10). The devil stands before God 24/7, accusing us of our past mistakes.

A demonic double take, then, is basing your future on your past. You messed up so many times earlier in your life that you believe you'll never change. Your disgraceful past and your hopeless future rob you of any peace in the present.

People tend to beat themselves up over their mistakes and sins. If you're beating yourself up, you're partnering with the Accuser in erasing your legacy. He loves it when you hurt yourself. He loves it when you say you can't do something.

The antidote to the demonic double take is to find something that Satan wants you to do, and don't do it. Or find something that Satan *doesn't* want you to do, and *do* it.

Secondly, you need to leave your past behind. Paul wrote in Philippians 3:13-14,

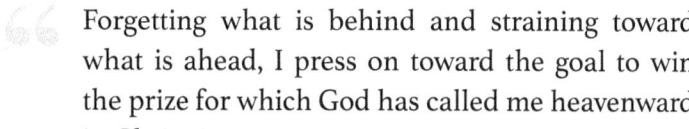

> Forgetting what is behind and straining toward what is ahead, I press on toward the goal to win the prize for which God has called me heavenward in Christ Jesus.

Of all people, Paul could have been hamstrung by the demonic double take because he participated in killing the early Christians (Acts 8:1). Nevertheless, he understood that God doesn't restrict our futures to the mistakes of our past.

Nor should you.

4. Make the most of every opportunity

Way back in the day, the ancient Greeks believed in a god named Kairos. With winged feet, muscle on muscle, long hair in front, and short hair in back, Kairos was the god of opportunity. According to Greek legend, he would stand next to a person, pause for a split second, and stare at him. If the person grabbed his long hair, Kairos would be the person's servant. But if the person hesitated, his winged feet would carry him away.

In Colossians 4:5, Paul wrote,

> Make the most of every *opportunity*" (italics added).

The Greek word for "opportunity" in this verse is *kairos*.

Make the most of every opportunity that comes your way—and remember that some opportunities look like interruptions. Like I mentioned in chapter 8, a friend of mine has a sign on his wall at work that says, "Interruptions are the ministry." I agree!

A lady in my neighborhood honks her horn at 6 o'clock every morning as she leaves for work, just to say goodbye to her dogs. She constantly talks about how lonely she feels. So our family goes over to her house every once in a while just to sit with her and talk. We're trying to make the most of every opportunity.

Another neighbor is in his 80s. He called out to me one day when I was running late and walking toward my car. Interruptions are the ministry, so I stopped, walked over to him, and sat down next to him. Then I called my kids to join us. Benjamin hopped onto his lap, and immediately the old man's face lit up. I don't know what difference our moment together will make in eternity, but he recently told me that he's been going to church a lot lately.

God presents us with *kairos* opportunities all the time. Be careful not to overlook them, because life can slip away like an hourglass. What may look like an interruption to others may very well be a *kairos* moment for you—an opportunity to minister to people's hearts.

5. Remember that it's never too late to change your legacy

Alfred Nobel didn't change his legacy until the last seven years of his life, when he was fifty-six years old. He changed his actions by giving his money to a trust that emphasized world peace. His changed action changed his reputation, which in turn changed his legacy.

Your changed actions will always change your reputation. There's no better time to change than right now. If you haven't been tithing—tithe. If you have not been complimenting your wife in public—start right now. If you haven't been sharing your faith—do it today! Every experience, every conversation, every change, is preparation for future ministry.

After hearing me speak at a Promise Keepers event, a man standing in the counseling line told me that he had come to the conference to cheat on his wife with a woman from that town. He started to sob when he told me that Jesus grabbed his heart that day and set him free from his bondage to sin and death. He said that he was going home, calling off the divorce, and committing himself to love his wife.

I call that building a legacy he can leave behind!

🧰 TOOL BOX

1. If you prayed to receive Jesus earlier in the chapter, then you need to get involved in a Bible-believing church. Ask around for recommendations of good evangelical churches in your area. After you being attending a church, ask the pastor to mentor you and help you grow in your faith.

2. To fuel your desire to share your faith, you need to share your faith!

3. Don't insult yourself when you mess up. The Lord doesn't like it when you insult someone else, and He doesn't like it when you insult yourself.

4. Every once in a while, ask God to show you why you're in your particular location. I bet He will show you an opportunity to minister to someone.

5. Any change in your life begins with an act of the will. You must want to change in order to change.

CONCLUSION

BECOMING THE MAN GOD CREATED YOU TO BE

A FEW YEARS AGO, I NEEDED TO BUILD A BRICK WALL TO SECURE the foundation to an addition I had built on my house. The wall was only one foot tall and ten feet wide—but it took me three stinking days to build! UGH!! Somehow, I couldn't get the mortar to cooperate. At first it was too soupy, so I added more concrete. Unfortunately, I added too much, so it hardened on me. This happened several times! Six months later the brick wall started showing cracks in the mortar.

As I walked down my street just a few days after finally finishing my wall, I saw a bricklayer bricking up the front of a house. While he stood on a scaffold, men from below threw bricks up to him. With rapid-fire precision, the mason snagged the bricks out of the air, applied mortar to them like an artist, and laid them in place. I sat on the ground and watched him in awe. What took him five minutes to accomplish took me three days!

Walking home, I realized that the Christian life is similar to the brick mason and me. You may know someone who has been living for God at full speed for years. He's like the bricklayer.

You, however, may just be starting out; and therefore you struggle to build a simple wall. Don't be discouraged. If you keep it up you will eventually become a brick mason.

The only way you will become the man God created you to be is by allowing Him to shape your character. Make knowing Him your greatest ambition. Pursue godly men who will train you and hold you accountable to grow—and ask them plenty of questions. Don't be satisfied with maintaining who you are.

As you grow in character, remember to serve God by using your spiritual gifts. Don't try to be someone else—be the man God created you to be. In the beginning you might look like me when I was trying to build my little brick wall. But over time you'll become a master bricklayer. You can do it!

Live Your Life on Purpose

Despite the medical breakthroughs over the last hundred years, mortality rates have remained remarkably unchanged. One out of every one men will die! You cannot escape your eventual death. Hebrews 9:27 tells us that we are "destined to die once, and after that to face judgment." You will either die or be raptured (that's a topic for another book)—either way, your mortal life will come to an end and you will stand before Jesus.

Wouldn't it be great to be welcomed into heaven and hear Jesus say, "Great job! I know at times your life got really hard, but you never gave up. Wait until you see what I have for you!"?

I'm sure you'd prefer that over "Why didn't you... ?"

One day while I was visiting some friends in their home, I saw a painting that touched my heart. I couldn't take my eyes off of it. Tears welled up in my eyes, and then my crying quickly turned from a sprinkle into a steady downpour. I couldn't stop sobbing.

Soon my friends dropped to their knees and began sobbing as well. To this day I'm not sure what happened, although people say that this painting has affected others in the same way.

God spoke to my heart that day. I knew God wanted this painting to symbolize my life. Since then I have tried to live my life based on the truth behind it.

Let me describe the painting to you. In the background was a rainbow, symbolizing God's covenant that He would never destroy the earth again by a flood (see Genesis 6–8). The background also included two silhouetted hands facing each other, with a dove in flight between the hands. The hands symbolized God and the dove symbolized the Holy Spirit.

In the foreground, two men were hugging each other. Apparently one of them had just died and was on his way to heaven. The man's head was buried in the chest of the other man—who was Jesus! Jesus was gripping the man tightly and smiling so big that you couldn't miss it. But what moved me so deeply was the tear running down Jesus' cheek. I couldn't take my eyes off the tear.

Someday I'm going to see Jesus face to face. I often wonder what it will be like. Will I drop to the ground in amazement? Will I grovel in the dirt? Will I sob? I want to hear Him say, "Well done, good and faithful servant."

I am living my life on purpose for that day! I am planning and strategizing for that meeting.

Friend, I hope you are living your life on purpose as well. My prayer is that you are planning and strategizing for that meeting.

I look forward to seeing you in heaven!

FORGE RESOURCES & OPPORTUNITIES

FORGE SPEAKERS & EVENTS
ForgeSpeakers.com

Needing someone to challenge your group to become passionate followers of Jesus who live with hearts on fire and lives on purpose? Book a Forge speaker for your next event!

FORGE EQUIPPING PROGRAMS for ALL AGES
ForgeForward.org/Equipping

Forge Equipping is not summer camp and training events "as usual." Forge challenges and equips people of all ages to become you-nique, lifelong Kingdom laborers in their everyday places.

FORGE BOOKS & RESOURCES
ForgeForward.org/Resources

Looking for a deeper relationship with God and practical ways to widen His Kingdom impact through your life? Forge has the resources you need.

THE FORGE APP
Essential Kingdom laboring tools right at your fingertips
TheForgeApp.org

JOIN THE MULTIPLYING MOVEMENT
Where everyday followers become Kingdom multipliers
MultiplyingMovements.com

FORGE VIDEO CONTENT
Subscribe to free video content at Youtube.com/ForgeForward

FORGE PODCAST
FuelForTheHarvest.com

FORGE DAILY TEXTS
Text SPARK to 33222 for one-sentence daily devotionals

NEEDING PRAYER?
Email us at Prayer@ForgeForward.org

CONTACT US
FORGE
14485 E. Evans Ave., Denver, Colorado 80014

303.745.8191
info@forgefoward.org